National Income and Employment Analysis

Introduction to Economics Series

Kenyon A. Knopf, *Editor*

ECONOMIC DEVELOPMENT AND GROWTH

Robert E. Baldwin

THE ECONOMICS OF POVERTY

Alan B. Batchelder

NATIONAL INCOME AND EMPLOYMENT ANALYSIS

Arnold Collery

INTERNATIONAL ECONOMIC PROBLEMS

James C. Ingram

THE MARKET SYSTEM

Robert H. Haveman and Kenyon A. Knopf

TOWARD ECONOMIC STABILITY

Maurice W. Lee

CASE STUDIES IN AMERICAN INDUSTRY

Leonard W. Weiss

National Income and Employment Analysis

ARNOLD COLLERY

Amherst College

John Wiley & Sons, Inc. New York · London · Sydney

Library of Congress Catalog Card Number: 66-16142
Printed in the United States of America

Introduction to Economics Series

Teachers of introductory economics seem to agree on the impracticality of presenting a comprehensive survey of economics to freshman or sophomores. Many of them believe there is a need for some alternative which provides a solid core of principles while permitting an instructor to introduce a select set of problems and applied ideas. This series attempts to fill that need and also to give the interested layman a set of self-contained books that he can absorb with interest and profit, without assistance.

By offering greater flexibility in the choice of topics for study, these books represent a more realistic and reasonable approach to teaching economics than most of the large, catchall textbooks. With separate volumes and different authors for each topic, the instructor is not as tied to a single track as in the omnibus introductory economics text.

Underlying the series is the pedagogical premise that students should be introduced to economics by learning how economists think about economic problems. Thus the concepts and relationships of elementary economics are presented to the student in conjunction with a few economic problems. An approach of this kind offers a good beginning to the student who intends to move on to advanced work and furnishes a clearer understanding for those whose study of economics is limited to an introductory exposure. Teachers and students alike should find the books helpful and stimulating.

Kenyon A. Knopf, Editor

Preface

Economics is a complex subject and is continually becoming more so. As a consequence, there is more to teach each year than there was before, and textbooks become longer and longer. And there is no end in sight.

An unfortunate result of this development is the increasing likelihood that students will become so bogged down in learning techniques and details that they will miss the really important points. It is interesting to know, for example, that a single bank which has received new reserves will not be able to lend as much as the banking system as a whole. But it is infinitely more important to know that, in an economy with mass unemployment, an increase in the money supply will not be simply inflationary. Too often students, in their struggle to master the first point and many others like it, come away from the study of economics without a proper understanding of the second.

The primary purpose of this text is to make this outcome less likely. The central issues of national income and employment analysis are brought into sharp focus. To insure that the beginning student understands the controversy that surrounds monetary and fiscal policy, many topics treated in other textbooks are omitted. What has been left out is not the difficult material, but some propositions of secondary and tertiary importance. As a consequence, many teachers will feel that supplementary reading is required, particularly for those taking the year-long elementary course. It is hoped, however, that having a skeletal presentation of national income analysis to work with, the student who puts flesh on the bones by additional reading will end up understanding the heart better than the toes.

A sound understanding of the modern treatment of any subject is enhanced by a knowledge of earlier treatments. One appreciates and has a better feel for the modern when one can compare and contrast it with the old. Since this is particularly true in economics, an attempt has been made to present not only modern analysis, but also the classical analysis. It should be emphasized that this is not done to disparage the thought of economists such as Adam Smith, David Ricardo, John Stuart Mill, Frederic Bastiat, and Alfred Marshall, but to enhance the student's understanding of modern analysis. Some of the conclusions presented in this book differ radically from those that were considered orthodox in the 1930s. It is important for the student to see why economists today hold views that differ from those of yesterday.

The first five chapters are self-contained. Their intention is to demonstrate that mass unemployment need not exist in a modern, capitalistic economy. In the first chapter, the classical approach to the problems of aggregate demand and employment is presented, and the assumptions on which it rested are shown to be questionable. The modern, Keynesian analysis of national income, which is based on slightly altered assumptions, is contained in Chapters 2 and 3. In Chapters 4 and 5, the implications of Keynesian analysis for monetary and fiscal policy are drawn.

The final two chapters might be omitted or read at a later point. They are there to indicate that, although full employment may be an attainable objective, it may not be possible to have full employment at zero cost. Difficult choices may have to be made. There is little point in convincing people that policies directed at the maintenance of prosperity are available unless they know the side effects. There may be a pill at hand that will cure a headache, but if it also blinds, no one in his right sense is going to take it. Chapter 6 discusses the possibility that full employment and stable prices may be incompatible objectives. Chapter 7 then deals with the further possibility that policies aimed at the maintenance of full employment may lead to balance-of-payments difficulties.

I am particularly indebted to James Kindahl of the University of Chicago and Heinz Köhler of Amherst College for reading most, if not all, of the manuscript. Their suggestions led to numerous changes. They are not responsible, however, for all of the remaining defects.

ARNOLD COLLERY

Contents

Glossary of Abbreviations

AC	Autonomous consumption demand
AD	Aggregate demand
AID	Autonomous investment demand
AS	Aggregate supply
AS	Autonomous saving
C	Consumption
CD	Consumption demand
CPT	Corporate profits taxes
D	Demand deposits of the public
DY	Disposable income
ER	Excess reserves of the commercial banks
G	Government expenditures
GBP	Gross business product
GD	Government demand
GNP	Gross national product
GPDI	Gross private domestic investment
GTP	Government transfer payments
HS	Household saving
IBT	Indirect business taxes
ID	Investment demand
IF	Indebtedness of the commercial banks to the federal reserve banks
LS	Loans and securities of commercial banks
M	Imports
MD	Import demand
mpc	Marginal propensity to consume
mpi	Marginal propensity to invest
mps	Marginal propensity to save
NI	Net investment
NNP	Net national product
NNP_e	Net national product in equilibrium
NNP_f	Net national product at full employment
NPDI	Net private domestic investment
NPI	Net private investment
NPS	Net private saving

NT	Net taxes
NW	Net worth of commercial banks
OA	Other assets of commercial banks
OL	Other liabilities of the commercial banks
PYT	Personal income taxes
r	Reserve requirement of the commercial banks
R	Reserves of the commercial banks
RE	Retained earnings
RR	Required reserves of the commercial banks
S	Saving
SST	Social security taxes
T	Taxes
X	Exports
XD	Export demand

National Income
and Employment Analysis

1

The Classical Theory of Employment

Unemployment has been one of the most damning characteristics of the American economy. There have been times in our society when men and women have been unable to work and earn a decent living for themselves and their families, even though our economy had great productive potential. People have been cold and hungry, in a land with a superabundance of coal, oil, and farmland. Young men and women have been deprived of an education in a land with unemployed teachers. People have had to do without the comforts of life, when our factories were idle. Men, able and willing to work, have experienced the degradation of living on charity.

What is the explanation of unemployment and depression? And what can we do about them? These are the questions that will be answered in this book. We want to know how it was possible in 1933 that 25% of the labor force was unemployed. We want to know so that our government can pursue policies to prevent it from ever happening again. We want to know so that when any unemployment does occur, when the economy becomes even slightly depressed, we shall be able to correct the situation.

I. VOLUNTARY UNEMPLOYMENT

Since this book is mostly about unemployment, we must be clear from the beginning about the meaning of this term. Just when is someone unemployed? Are housewives, who choose to stay at home, unemployed? Are college students, who spend their time attending classes and reading books, unemployed?

There is, of course, a sense in which housewives and students are unemployed; they are not working for a wage or salary. But no one would consider their unemployment a problem; they are not even in the labor force. If we wish to speak of them as being unemployed, we must say that they are *voluntarily unemployed,* since they do not choose to work for income.

Even if someone asserts that he wants to work, he may still be voluntarily unemployed. If he is only willing to accept a job for which he is not qualified or only willing to accept work at a wage greater than that currently earned by persons with his skills and abilities, he is voluntarily unemployed. If John Smith could find a job driving a truck (if he were trained for nothing else) and if he insisted that the only job he would take was acting in television plays or if he insisted that he would not drive a truck for less than $50,000 a year, he would be voluntarily unemployed. John Smith and people like him are not the concern of this book.

II. INVOLUNTARY UNEMPLOYMENT

It may happen that someone is ready, willing, and able to work at the going wage for workers with his skills and experience and yet is unable to find employment. Such a person is involuntarily unemployed.

A certain amount of involuntary unemployed is normal in our economy; normal in the sense that we always expect to have it. It is the price that we pay for change. If an economy is dynamic—and we would not want to live in one that was not—some involuntary unemployment is almost inevitable. Technological change and shifting demands can cause temporary unemployment. More efficient methods of production may lead to a reduction in the amount of labor required to produce some product; some workers may lose their jobs. But more efficient techniques may result in a demand for labor elsewhere. When these occur simultaneously, jobs exist for the unemployed. However, until those out of work find the jobs that are available, they are unemployed. The same situation can occur when the demand for one product rises while the demand for another falls. If people suddenly want more shoes and fewer coats, some involuntary unemployment is likely. The output of coats will fall, and fewer workers will be needed to make them. But the increase in demand for shoes will lead to an increase in demand for labor. Until the unemployed workers find the jobs that are available in the economy, they are involuntarily unemployed. Involuntary unemployment stemming from changing technology or shifting demand together with voluntary unemployment stemming from people moving from one job to a better one are called *frictional unemployment.*

Frictional unemployment need not be a serious problem in our society. When unemployment is entirely of this kind, there are jobs for all. The government might wish to grant temporary unemployment assistance and to spread information about job opportunities, but there is no need to create jobs because there is enough work for everyone who wants it.

This book is not about frictional unemployment; our main concern is with nonfrictional, involuntary unemployment. We wish to understand a situation in which, if every employer filled every vacancy, there would still be people looking for work. When we speak of unemployment throughout this book, unless we specify to the contrary, we shall always mean nonfrictional, involuntary unemployment.

QUESTIONS

1. Are the following people voluntarily or involuntarily unemployed? If your answer is involuntarily, specify whether their unemployment should be labeled frictional or nonfrictional.

   (a) Mr. Smith was a college professor for 45 years and, having reached the mandatory retirement age, has moved to Florida where he spends his days reading and writing for pleasure.

   (b) Mrs. Smith, who has never worked for money, finds that her husband's retirement income is less than she desires. For $10 an hour she is willing to arrange flowers or advise young wives on how to serve tea, but has found no employment.

   (c) Mr. Johns has been laid off. His former employer has experienced a sharp reduction in sales as a result of a decline in consumer interest in his product. There are many firms, experiencing increasing demand, and they are advertising for people with Mr. Johns' training and skills.

   (d) Mr. Doe has been laid off from his $9000 a year job as a foreman in an automobile factory. The demand for cars has fallen, as has the demand for everything else except bankruptcy forms. Mr. Doe is willing to accept a job similar to the one that he had, at less money than others who are no more qualified are currently earning. He has looked everywhere, and has even offered to take less skilled work, but can find no satisfactory job. Someone did offer him a job baby-sitting at 40¢ an hour, but he refused it.

(e) Mrs. Brown is a widow with six children who are under the age of eight. She would be willing to take any job at any wage, if she could only find someone to take care of her children. But no one has offered to do so.

2. Can an employed person be poor?
3. If no involuntary unemployment ever existed, would we be living in Utopia?

III. IS A GAP BETWEEN INCOME AND OUTPUT RESPONSIBLE FOR UNEMPLOYMENT?

There have been numerous attempts to explain involuntary, non-frictional unemployment. One of the least defensible ones maintains that unemployment is inevitable, since the economy, left to itself, produces more output than income to buy the output. According to this view, if everyone were given a job, the payments of income to the factors of production would not be enough to buy all that was produced. If an output of $100 worth of goods and services were produced during a period, the purchasing power created to buy that output might be only $80. Even if everyone spent all of his income, all that has been produced could not be sold. Unemployment would then be inevitable, since business firms would not go on hiring labor to produce goods that they could not sell.

In order to show why this is a bad argument, we must understand exactly how income and output are related. Can income ever be less than output? To answer this question, we must first develop some standard accounting concepts. And we begin with a definition of profits.

Profits = sales − all the costs of making the goods and services sold

Rewriting this statement, we have

Sales = all the costs of making the goods and services sold + profits

Now imagine an economy in which there is only one firm, no government, and no foreign trade. We can call this economy the Land of Simplicity. A profit-and-loss statement for the Monopoly business firm in Simplicity is presented in Table 1-1. Having defined profits as the difference between sales and the costs of the goods and services sold, the sum of the items on the right-hand side necessarily equals that of the left, as it does in the statement.

Table 1-1. Profit-and-Loss Statement of the Monopoly Firm in the Land of Simplicity

Sales to households (consumption)	$100	Costs of the goods and services sold:	
		Wages and salaries	$70
		Rent	4
		Interest	10
		Depreciation	9
		Profits	7
Total sales	$100	Total costs plus profits	$100

The profit-and-loss statement contains information about sales and costs for a period of time, but it does not tell us about production. The firm may have produced goods that it did not sell, or it might have sold goods that were produced in an earlier period. If the firm in Simplicity has sold goods entirely from inventories, its production may have been very small or even nothing. If it added goods to inventories or built new capital facilities for itself, then its production was greater than its sales.

QUESTIONS

1. Given the following information for a firm during a period of time, prepare a profit-and-loss statement.

Sales	$400
Wages and salaries	350
Rent	15
Interest	30
Depreciation	40

2. Why must sales, without any exceptions whatever, equal the sum of costs of producing the goods sold and profits?

IV. THE PRODUCTION STATEMENT

What we seek is a "production statement" rather than a profit-and-loss statement. The profit-and-loss statement can be converted into a production statement by adding to the left-hand side the value of the capital goods that have been produced during the period (new buildings and equipment) and any changes in inventories that occurred. If the goods produced but not sold are valued at their costs of production, we can add these costs to the right-hand side.

Imagine, for example, that the Monopoly firm in Simplicity built new buildings and equipment worth $24 and added $3 worth of goods to its inventories. The $24 figure and the $3 figure are found by adding together all the costs that were incurred by making these goods. If we then adjust the profit-and-loss statement in order to include the goods that have been produced but not sold, we have the new statement given in Table 1-2.

Table 1-2. Production Statement for the Monopoly Firm in Simplicity

Sales to households (consumption)	$100	Costs of the goods and services sold:	
New buildings and equipment manufactured	24	Wages and salaries	$70
Additions to inventories	3	Rent	4
		Interest	10
		Depreciation	9
		Costs of the goods produced but not sold:	
		Wages and salaries	$20
		Rent	1
		Interest	2
		Depreciation	4
		Profits	7
	$127		$127

If we combine the costs, adding together the costs of the goods and services sold and the costs of the goods and services produced but not sold, we will have the costs of all the goods and services produced during the period. The production statement would then be as shown in Table 1-3.

Table 1-3. Production Statement for the Monopoly Firm in Simplicity

Sales to households (consumption)	$100	Costs of the goods and services produced:	
New buildings and equipment manufactured	24	Wages and salaries	$90
Additions to inventories	3	Rent	5
		Interest	12
		Depreciation	13
		Profits	7
GNP	$127	GNP	$127

Assuming that no production occurs within households, Simplicity's Gross National Product (GNP) is $127, since that is the total output of all final goods and services. The Net National Product (NNP) can be obtained from the GNP by subtracting depreciation. NNP is $114.

NNP is a better measure of an economy's production than the GNP. If a nation continually consumed its entire gross national product, and all sales were to households, it would never build new buildings and equipment; it would never replace its capital as it wore out. An economy that did not maintain its capital would eventually become poorer and poorer. GNP is not a good measure, therefore, of how much a country could consume without becoming worse off. A nation could consume its NNP, without becoming poorer, however. If consumption equaled NNP, firms would be producing just enough capital to replace what is wearing away; the value of new buildings and equipment would equal depreciation.

The net-national-product statement for Simplicity is as given in Table 1-4:

Table 1-4. Net-National-Product Statement, Land of Simplicity

Sales to households (consumption)	$100	Wages and salaries	$90
New buildings and equipment minus depreciation (net additions to buildings and equipment)	11	Rent	5
Changes in inventories	3	Interest	12
		Profits	7
Net national product	$114	Net national product	$114

There are two ways to measure a nation's net national product: sum up either the items on the left-hand side or the right-hand side of its net-national-product statement. NNP is equal to the sum of consumption, net additions to buildings and equipment, and change in inventories, and it is also equal to the sum of all wages and salaries, rent, interest, and profits.

Each of the items on the right-hand side of the NNP statement is a kind of income, and there is no kind of income not listed there. These items added together, therefore, constitute the national income of Simplicity. The net national product and the national income are the same.

There is nothing mysterious or surprising about this. In producing the NNP, the Monopoly firm in Simplicity had to pay wages and salaries, rent, and interest. Since the value of the product produced exceeded the sum of these costs, it made a profit—a profit equal to the difference between them. When that profit is added to the other incomes (wages and salaries, rent, and interest), the sum of all of the incomes is necessarily equal to the product produced.

Having established a necessary equality between NNP and national income, we can now deal with the problem introduced at the beginning of this section. Can unemployment be explained by a failure of the economy to generate enough income in the process of production to permit people to buy all that has been produced? Of course, the answer is no. We have just learned that the national income is necessarily equal to the net national product; income equals output. Since this is true, unemployment cannot be caused by a gap between income and output. Nonfrictional, involuntary unemployment must have some other explanation.

QUESTIONS

1. Given the information below for the Monopoly firm in Simplicity, prepare a production statement similar to the one given in Table 1-4.

Sales	$200
Wages and salaries for goods sold	140
Rent for goods sold	10

Interest for goods sold	20
Depreciation incurred in producing goods sold	30
Additions to buildings and equipment	30
Wages and salaries paid to manufacture buildings and equipment	20
Rent incurred to manufacture buildings and equipment	4
Interest incurred to manufacture buildings and equipment	2
Depreciation incurred to manufacture buildings and equipment	4
Change in inventories	−15
Wages and salaries paid on goods sold from inventories	10
Rent paid on goods sold from inventories	2
Interest paid on goods sold from inventories	1
Depreciation incurred on goods sold from inventories	2

2. Alter the production statement in Question 1 so that profits will exist.
3. Using the information given in Question 1, prepare a net-national-product statement.
4. If NNP is $95 and depreciation $5, what is GNP?
5. What is wrong with the following statement?

Socialism is inevitable; it cannot be stopped. Under capitalism, production chronically exceeds the income that people have to buy what is produced. Crises and depressions recur again and again. Eventually the people are bound to cast-off this absurd system and seize the means of production. Then they will distribute all that is produced to the workers, and income will always equal output. Crises, depressions, and unemployment will be no more, for their cause will be no more.

V. IS SAVING RESPONSIBLE FOR UNEMPLOYMENT?

Although unemployment cannot be explained by a failure of the economy to generate enough income to buy output, there is another possible explanation. People may not spend all of their incomes. Even though income is sufficient to buy all the output, the income may not be used to do so.

VI. SAVING IN A BARTER ECONOMY

Although it remains to be seen whether saving could cause unemployment in an economy with money, in an economy without financial assets such as money, it could not. If there were no financial assets, business would be conducted by barter; one good would be exchanged for another. In a barter economy, involuntary, nonfrictional unemployment could not result from a failure of people to spend their incomes. All the factors of production would be paid in goods and services. If the public did not wish to consume its entire income, it would still have to demand goods in order to save. There is nothing one can do with his income but consume goods and services, or hold goods.

Frictional unemployment would be possible in a barter economy, nonetheless. If people wanted fewer shoes and more hats, the value of shoes would fall and the value of hats would rise. It would, no longer, be possible to get as many hats or other things for shoes, but at the same time hats would exchange for more of other things. With the fall in the value of shoes, shoe production would become less profitable, and the production of shoes would decrease; labor would become unemployed. But if shoe production is less profitable, hat production is more profitable. The output of hats would rise as producers of hats hired more labor. The movement in demand away from shoes and toward hats would result in unemployment, temporarily. But it would be frictional unemployment; there would still be jobs for everyone who is ready, willing, and able to work.

QUESTIONS

1. In an economy without money or other financial assets, in what form would people receive their income?
2. If you did not want to consume all of your income, what would you do with the rest?
3. When people supply shoes, they must demand something for them. If there are more shoes supplied than demanded, why must there be more demand than supply of something else?

VII. SAVING IN A MONETARY ECONOMY

The above analysis is, of course, highly artificial. No economy of any complexity can function without money. People who have argued that saving is responsible for unemployment have not assumed an imaginary economy without money; they were talking about an economy in which money is used to buy and sell goods and services.

Can saving in an economy that uses money cause unemployment? It is true that some saving usually does occur; people do not spend all of their income on consumer goods. To be able to consume more in the future, or to have a nest egg, or simply out of habit, many people in our society save part of their income. Can the failure of consumption to equal output be responsible for unemployment in a monetary economy?

Classical economists always said no. They believed that what was true of a barter economy was also true of a money economy. There could never be deficient demand. According to them, income that is not consumed—not spent on bread and butter—is spent nonetheless, since no one would ever hold any of his savings in the form of money. If the national income were $100, people might only spend $85 buying consumer goods; saving would be $15. But the $15 saved would not be idle; it would not be hoarded. If the savers themselves did not have a use for it, if they did not want to invest in a house or a machine or some other form of capital, then they would lend it to someone else who did. According to the classical writers, no saver would fail to put his savings back into circulation, since idle money would earn no interest, while money invested in houses or machines or money lent to others would.

VIII. CLASSICAL WRITERS EXAGGERATED THE WILLINGNESS OF PEOPLE TO SPEND OR LEND THEIR SAVINGS

It is certainly true that people do not hold all of their savings in the form of money. Most people use most of their savings most of the time to buy capital or to lend to others. But the classical proposition states that *all* of the people *all* of the time use *all* of their savings for these purposes. And that simply is not true. *Some* people *some* of the time hold *some* of their savings in the form of money. Therefore, not all that is saved is spent.

Even if every saver either spent or lent all that he has saved, it still need not follow that all that is saved is spent, that saving cannot lead to unemployment. Imagine, for example, that people place part of their savings into savings banks. The savings banks tend to lend out what has been deposited with them to those who wish to invest. But they may not lend out new deposits fully. In fact, in our economy, most banks are required to keep money as a reserve against deposits. The more money they owe, the more money they have to have on hand. If income and output were $100 during a year and if people saved $20 from their incomes and placed it in savings deposits, the banks would then be able to lend, but not $20. If they were required to have a money reserve of 5% against savings deposits, they would be able to lend $19, but not $20. Since this is true, all that is saved would not be spent. If it were, someone would be breaking the law.

In addition to spending or putting their savings into a savings bank, people may buy stocks and bonds. If the money is used to buy new stocks and bonds, the corporations selling the stocks and bonds may not spend all of the money that they receive. As a business expands it needs more cash on hand to make sure it can always meet its obligations. The bigger the business, the more money it holds. When a business floats new securities in order to grow, it is likely to spend only a portion of the proceeds. Although the portion spent may be large, some of the money would become idle, and all that has been saved would not be spent.

Finally, even if people did not initially wish to hold money, but preferred to use their savings to buy capital goods or to lend, they might in the end decide to hold money anyway. Imagine, for example, that the community has saved $15 out of a national income of $100. If the savers, themselves, invest $5 of their savings in buying capital goods, there would then be a problem of finding others to borrow and invest $10. But it may happen that investors do not want to borrow and spend

$10. If they wished to borrow and spend only $8, there would be an excess of money available equal to $2.

When people are trying to lend more than people are trying to borrow, competition reduces interest rates. Lower interest rates encourage people to borrow to buy capital, capital that they previously thought too expensive. If interest rates fell enough, the excess $2 would be borrowed and invested. But as interest rates fall, some of the savers may decide that they would just as soon keep all or part of their savings in money. At the old interest rates they were willing to lend it all, but with interest rates having fallen, they decide to hang on to some of their money, the interest they can now earn being too little to make lending all of their savings worthwhile. When this occurs, all that has been saved is not spent, as the classical economists believed, and saving might be a problem.

QUESTIONS

1. In the real world, what are the forms in which an individual can keep his savings?
2. Why did the classical economists believe that no one would ever keep his savings in money?
3. Why, even if all savers place all of their savings into savings banks, will investors be unable to spend all that has been saved?
4. If people are trying to lend $50, while people are trying to borrow only $20, what would tend to happen to interest rates? Why would a decrease in interest rates encourage some to borrow more? Why would a decrease in interest rates encourage some to hold all or part of their savings in the form of money?

IX. HOW THE CLASSICAL ECONOMISTS MIGHT ANSWER

Although the classical economists did not analyze this problem with enough care to realize that saving might not lead to an equal amount of spending on capital goods, they would still be able to argue that unemployment, other than of a frictional type, would never exist. How was this possible?

In the 18th and 19th centuries the connection between gold and the money supply was much closer than it is now. This makes a difference. To see why, imagine that in Simplicity all money consists of gold coins. The government of Simplicity has declared that one ounce of gold is worth $50. If anyone brings an ounce of gold to the mint, the government will form it into a disc and will stamp on it $50, legal tender for all debts public and private. Assume, further, that no gold is currently being mined in Simplicity because the cost of doing so just exceeds the value of gold; it costs slightly more than $50 to mine an ounce of gold.

If part of Simplicity's national income is saved and if savers fail to buy capital themselves or if they fail to get their savings into the hands of those who wish to buy capital, this would indicate a desire on the savers' part to hold some of their wealth in the form of money. All that is saved is not spent; part is hoarded. In an ideal community when the people wish to hold more money, more money would become available. Is this all that would happen in Simplicity, or would a depression and unemployment occur?

A classical economist could say that when people wished to hold more money, more money would be produced. The failure of the people of Simplicity to buy all that is produced would lead to an undesired accumulation of inventories; all that is produced would not be sold. Businessmen would lessen their output and, as they did, they would lay off workers. In order to maintain their jobs, some of the workers would offer to work for less; wages would fall. But if wages are reduced, the cost of production decreases, and firms, actively competing with one another, would have to lower their prices. All prices would tend to fall, except one. Remember that the price of gold is fixed by the government of Simplicity at $50 an ounce.

As the factors of production became cheaper, gold mining would become more profitable. At the old wage rates, it did not pay to mine gold, but with wages down, it would now be profitable to do so. Labor would be hired in the gold industry, and the money supply would expand, since the producers of gold would take their output to the government to have it minted into coins.

We thus see that the economy would respond as, ideally, it should; the public wished to have more money, so resources were then taken from producing shoes and butter and put into the production of gold, which is money. If the people of Simplicity wished to save $15 out of a national income of $100, and if they wished neither to spend $5 of their saving on investment goods nor to lend it to others to spend on investment goods, the desire to hoard would not cause any permanent problem. If wages and prices fell enough to stimulate gold production to the extent of $5, everything would be all right.

Imagine, for example, that the economy produces $85 worth of consumer goods (shoes and butter), $5 worth of gold, and $10 worth of new buildings and equipment. The output and national income in Simplicity would be $100. Consumers spend $85 on the consumer goods and lend to investors $10, which they spend on the new buildings and equipment. The producers of all goods find that they are able to sell all that they have produced; there is no longer any reason to lay off workers—full employment would prevail.

But gold is not so important any longer in our economy. Most of our money supply consists of unbacked pieces of paper and bank deposits. What would happen, in this case, if spending were not equal to the national output and income? What happens if people wish to hoard in an economy in which gold or some other commodity cannot be turned into money?

Even in this instance, unemployment would eventually cure itself, if the economy were competitive. Imagine that the entire money supply consists of pieces of paper issued by the government of Simplicity. Assume, also, that spending fails to equal income; hoarding occurs. If businessmen gave jobs to everyone, they would be unable to sell all that they produced because all that is saved is not spent buying capital goods. They would, therefore, lay off some of their workers. But if wages and prices are competitively determined, the unemployed workers would agree to work for less money. With wages down, competition would force down prices also. In our earlier example, where money was gold, the deflation of prices stimulated the production of gold and an expansion of the money supply. But in this case, money consists of pieces of paper issued by the government. Unless the government decided to print more money, the money supply would not grow, no matter how much wages and prices fell.

Does that mean that businessmen would never be able to sell all that is produced, if they gave a job to everybody who wanted to work? The answer is no. As prices fell, the purchasing power of each piece of paper would become greater. Those holding the paper money would discover that their money has increased in purchasing power. With $10 you can buy a certain quantity of goods and services; your money has a certain purchasing power. But if prices are cut in half and if you still have the $10, you can buy twice as many goods and services; the purchasing power of your money has doubled.

As the purchasing power of money increased, as people became richer and richer, spending would increase. Although people might not be willing to buy all that can be produced when shoes are selling for $4 a pair and butter for 50¢ a pound, at some lower level of prices (for instance, shoes selling for $2 a pair and butter for 25¢ a pound), people would have so much more purchasing power that they would buy all that is produced.

We can see, therefore, that the classical economists were right, in a sense, to believe that unemployment would always tend to cure itself. If the economy is highly competitive, unemployment can always be considered frictional. When firms cannot sell all that is being produced, wages and prices fall. The deflation of wages and prices either expands the production of gold or simply increases the purchasing power of money until people buy the total production of the economy.

The classical view is clearly correct if the assumptions are correct. But are the assumptions correct? Do wages and prices fall when people are unemployed?

QUESTIONS

1. Assume that the government is prepared to buy and sell unlimited quantities of a certain kind of pencil at 4¢ each. When it buys $1000 worth of pencils, it prints up $1000 worth of paper money to pay for them. When it sells $1000 worth of pencils it destroys the paper money that has been paid for them. If, initially, the government were neither buying nor selling pencils, what would happen in the economy if hoarding occurred (people do not spend all of their income to buy goods and services, they try to add to their money balances)?

2. Assume that people are holding $200 billion worth of paper money. If prices fall by 25%, why would they be richer? If people are richer, are they likely to buy more goods and services? Explain, then, why unemployment would tend to cure itself.

X. WAGES AND PRICES IN THE GREAT DEPRESSION

There is substantial evidence that our economy is not competitive enough for the classical theory to be applicable. In many of our industries, wages are determined by the bargaining of unions and management, and the unions are not prepared to accept wage cuts just because there is unemployment. Furthermore, some wages are determined by the Congress of the United States, since it fixes the minimum wage. If there were unemployment, that wage could only fall if the Congress were prepared to lower the minimum, which it probably would not do.

In addition, prices in many industries are not likely to fall just because demand goes down and costs fall. Firms avoid price competition as much as possible, and some are able to resist price reductions. If the demand for cars or steel falls next year, almost no one would be surprised if prices rose rather than fell. Excess capacity and unemployment in these industries does not automatically lead to wage and price reductions.

Table 1-5 reports information on wages, prices, and unemployment in the United States during the great depression. Notice what happened to the cost of living in the United States from 1933 until 1937. It rose by 11%. But, during this same period of time, from 18 to 25% of the labor force was unemployed. With absolutely massive unemployment in our economy, prices actually rose rather than fell. It ought to be clear to everyone that we cannot rely on wage and price reductions to cure unemployment.

XI. JOHN MAYNARD KEYNES AND THE GENERAL THEORY OF EMPLOYMENT INTEREST AND MONEY

In 1936 the great English economist, John Maynard Keynes, published a book called *The General Theory of Employment Interest and Money*. Keynes argued that wages and prices no longer fall, even with extensive unemployment. He believed

Table 1-5.

Year	Unemployment as Per Cent of the Civilian Labor Force	Average Gross Hourly Earnings in Manufacturing	Consumer Price Indexes 1947—1949 = 100
1929	3.2	$0.566	73.3
1930	8.7	0.552	71.4
1931	15.9	0.515	65.0
1932	23.6	0.446	58.4
1933	24.9	0.442	55.3
1934	21.7	0.532	57.2
1935	20.1	0.550	58.7
1936	16.9	0.556	59.3
1937	14.3	0.624	61.4
1938	19.0	0.627	60.3
1939	17.2	0.633	59.4
1940	14.6	0.661	59.9
1941	9.9	0.729	62.9
1942	4.7	0.853	69.7
1943	1.9	0.961	74.0

Source. Department of Labor.

that it was necessary to reconsider the classical economic theories, since they assumed that competition would lead to wage and price declines and automatically cure any tendency for unemployment. He undertook the task of explaining what would happen when hoarding occurs in a world in which wages and prices will not decline.

Keynes' theory is complicated, and his book is not easy to read. In the next few chapters we shall give what many consider to be the gist of his analysis.

QUESTIONS

1. Average hourly earnings in manufacturing rose every year between 1933 and 1940. Do you believe that these wage increases can be explained by saying that the demand for labor was greater than the supply in each of these years?
2. "Although wages and prices did not fall rapidly during the 1930's, as would have been required for the automatic, free-enterprise mechanism to eliminate unemployment quickly, if the government had left things alone and if the war had not intervened, eventually the classical mechanism would have come into play. Unemployed

workers would have undercut union labor; and wages would have fallen; new business firms would have entered to compete with the old, and prices would have fallen. It might have taken several decades, possibly as much as fifty years, for the depression to cure itself, but it would have eventually. Keynes and his followers were just too impatient. They had no business advocating government action to cure unemployment when *eventually* unemployment would have been cured without government intervention." Do you agree?

XII. SUMMARY

1. Unemployment is either voluntary or involuntary. A person is involuntarily unemployed if he is ready, willing, and able to work at the going wage for workers with his skills and abilities and is yet unable to find employment.

2. Involuntary unemployment can be classified as frictional or nonfrictional. Involuntary, frictional unemployment exists when there are sufficient jobs for everyone; an oversupply of labor at one place is balanced by an undersupply somewhere else. If an economy is dynamic, frictional unemployment is inevitable. Nonfrictional, involuntary unemployment occurs when there are fewer jobs than people who are looking for work.

3. Since this book is mainly about nonfrictional, involuntary unemployment, one of our major tasks is to explain how such unemployment can occur. One explanation that has been offered is logically invalid. It holds that the economy simply does not create enough income in the process of production to make it possible to buy all that is produced. Profits, however, are the difference between the NNP and wages and salaries, rent, and interest, paid out as a result of production. When profits are added to these other incomes, we see that the total of all incomes (wages and salaries, rents, interest, and profits) is, necessarily, equal to the NNP. Income cannot be less than output because it is, necessarily, equal to it.

4. Others have argued that unemployment is caused by a failure of people to spend all of their income; saving is the villain. In a barter economy this would not be a problem, since the only thing you can do with your income is demand goods and services; there is nothing else. The classical economists

asserted that what was true in a barter economy was also true in a monetary economy. They believed that all saving would be used to buy capital goods. If savers did not wish to buy such goods themselves, then they would lend their savings to others who would do so. According to them, saving never results in a desire to hold more money.

5. But this view is not correct. *Some* people *some* of the time hold *some* of their savings in the form of money. In addition, some savings get placed in banks, and the banks hold a reserve in money against the deposits; they do not lend out all that has been saved and deposited with them. Moreover, if savers use their funds to buy new stocks and bonds, the corporations who receive the money may hold part of it; the larger the business the more money it holds. Finally, saving may result in more funds being available for lending than people wish to borrow. When this happens, interest rates tend to fall. But when interest rates fall, some people will decide to keep some of their saving in money and not lend it out. The cost and inconvenience of lending may be too great compared to income that can be earned at the lowered interest rates.

6. The classical economists could argue that even if people do not spend themselves or lend to those who wish to spend all of their savings, involuntary, nonfrictional unemployment would still not occur. If our economy were highly competitive and if we were on a rigid gold standard, with all money consisting of gold, any failure of spending to equal the NNP would result in wage reductions and price reductions, except for the price of gold which is fixed by the government. As costs fell, gold production would become more profitable, and unemployed labor would be absorbed into the gold industry. If we were on a pure paper-money standard, a failure of spending to equal NNP would again lead to wage and prices reductions in a competitive economy. But, in this case, there would be no gold industry to absorb the unemployed. Wages and prices would not fall forever, nonetheless. As prices fell, the purchasing power of the fixed money supply would grow, and people would feel richer. Being richer they would spend more on consumer goods. Prices would fall until total spending equaled the NNP.

7. The classical argument depends on the assumption that wages and prices will fall if there is unemployment. But this does not necessarily happen in our economy. There were years in the 1930's when wages and prices rose, even though there was massive unemployment.

8. Since the assumptions of the classical theory are not valid today, we need a more realistic theory, one that assumes that wages do not fall when there is unemployment. Such a theory was developed by John Maynard Keynes. The basic elements of that theory and its implications will be given in the following chapters.

2

The Bare Elements of the Keynesian Theory

In the previous chapter we established an NNP statement for an economy with only a single firm. Let us take one step toward greater realism by acknowledging that there are many firms in our economy. Does this fact essentially alter the NNP statement?

Although the introduction of many firms adds complications, it does not alter the NNP statement. Things become more complicated because the production statement of a firm may no longer indicate its real productive activity; it may use the product of some other firm in producing its output. A shoe factory may make and sell 1000 pairs of shoes. If the shoes sell for $5.00 a pair, one cannot conclude that it has produced $5000 worth of output. The shoes contain leather that was produced by others. The shoe factories output of shoes is not, therefore, its real contribution to the production of the economy; its contribution is less than that.

I. PRODUCTION IN AN ECONOMY WITH THREE FIRMS

The complications introduced by the existence of many firms can be understood by imagining a hypothetical economy consisting of three firms; a firm that produces goods and services for consumers, a firm that produces buildings and equipment, and a firm that produces raw materials. Their production statements might appear as shown in Table 2-1.

Table 2-1.

Production Statement, Consumer-Goods Firm

Sales to consumers	$115	Wages and salaries	$70
Changes in inventories	+5	Rent	5
		Interest	3
		Depreciation	10
		Purchases of raw materials	30
		Profits	2
	$120		$120

Production Statement, Capital-Goods Firm

Sales to consumer-goods firm	$15	Wages and salaries	$19
		Rent	1
Sales to raw-materials firm	9	Interest	5
Additions to buildings and equipment	12	Depreciation	4
		Purchases of raw materials	3
Changes in inventories	+4	Profits	8
	$40		$40

Production Statement, Raw-Materials Firm

Sales to consumer-goods firm	$30	Wages and salaries	$18
Sales to capital-goods firm	3	Rent	1
Changes in inventories	—2	Interest	2
		Depreciation	6
		Profits	4
	$31		$31

The production statement for the consumer-goods firm and the capital-goods firm differ slightly from the production statement in the previous chapter. A new item appears on the right-hand side; it is *purchases of raw materials.* If there is only one firm, as we assumed in the previous chapter, this item cannot appear, since there is no other firm to sell the Monopoly firm raw materials.

The production statement for the consumer-goods firm shows an output of $120; it sold $115 worth of goods and services to consumers, and added $5 worth to its inventories. But it did not, itself, create $120 worth of output, since it bought $30 worth of raw materials. Contained in its production of $120 are

$30 worth of goods that were produced elsewhere. Its contribution to the production of the community was actually $90.

The true output of the capital-goods firm is not $40. Contained in its ostensible output are $3 worth of raw materials that were produced elsewhere. Its contribution to GNP was actually $37.

Since the raw-materials firm did not buy raw materials from any other firm, its production was $31, as shown on its production statement. It sold $33 worth of goods, but its inventories fell by $2. Therefore, it produced $31 worth of goods during the period.

QUESTIONS

1. What has the firm, whose production statement appears below, contributed to GNP?

Production Statement for Firm X

Sales to consumers	$450	Wages and salaries	$ 25
		Purchases of raw materials	450
		Profits	—25
	$450		$450

II. THE VALUE-ADDED STATEMENT

If we subtract the purchases of raw materials from each side of the production statement, we will have a new statement; it is called the "value-added statement." It is a true indication of a firm's contribution to the GNP. The value-added statements for the three firms are as given in Table 2-2.

Table 2-2.

Value-Added Statement, Consumer-Goods Firm

Sales to consumers	$115	Wages and salaries	$70
Changes in inventories	5	Rent	5
(Minus) Purchases of raw materials	—30	Interest	3
		Depreciation	10
		Profits	2
	$ 90		$90

Table 2-2. (*cont.*)

Value-Added Statement, Capital-Goods Firm

Sales to consumer-goods firm	$15	Wages and salaries	$19
Sales to raw-materials firm	9	Rent	1
Additions to buildings and equipment	12	Interest	5
Changes in inventories	4	Depreciation	4
(Minus) Purchases of raw materials	—3	Profits	8
	$37		$37

Value-Added Statement, Raw-Materials Firm

Sales to consumer-goods firm	$30	Wages and salaries	$18
Sales to capital-goods firm	3	Rent	1
Changes in inventories	—2	Interest	2
		Depreciation	6
		Profits	4
	$31		$31

QUESTIONS

1. From the production statement below, prepare the value-added statement.

Production Statement

Sales to consumers	$75	Wages and salaries	$ 80
Sales to businesses	50	Rent	50
Sales to government	225	Interest	25
		Depreciation	20
		Purchases of raw materials	105
		Profits	70
	$350		$350

III. THE GROSS BUSINESS PRODUCT STATEMENT

The gross product created within the business sector (GBP) consists of the sum of the *values added* by all of the firms in the economy. GBP does not consist of the sum of what is loosely called the *production* of each firm, since that would count the same goods more than once. The output of shoes would be added to the output of leather and the output of cattle, but part of the output of leather is already contained in the output of shoes. GBP would be $158 in our hypothetical economy. This number is found by adding together the sums at the bottom of each of the value-added statements ($90 + $37 + $31).

Combining all of the value-added statements, we obtain a GBP statement. In our example, it is as shown in Table 2-3.

Table 2-3. Statement of Gross Product Created Within Business Sector in Absence of Government and Foreign Trade

Sales to consumers	$115	Consumer-goods firm:	
Changes in the inventories of the consumer-goods firm	5	Wages and salaries	$ 70
(Minus) Purchases of raw materials by the consumer-goods firm	—30	Rent	5
Sales to the consumer-goods firm by the capital-goods firm	15	Interest	3
Sales to the raw-materials firm by the capital-goods firm	9	Depreciation	10
Additions to buildings and equipment in the capital-goods firm	12	Profits	2
Changes in the inventories of the capital-goods firm	4	Capital-goods firm:	
(Minus) Purchases of raw materials by the capital-goods firm	—3	Wages and salaries	19
Sales to the consumer goods firm by the raw-materials firm	30	Rent	1
Sales to the capital-goods firm by the raw-materials firm	3	Interest	5
Changes in inventories in the raw-materials firm	—2	Depreciation	4
		Profits	8
		Raw-materials firm:	
		Wages and salaries	18
		Rent	1
		Interest	2
		Depreciation	6
		Profits	4
Gross business product:	$158	Gross business product:	$158

This gross-business-product statement can be simplified considerably. (1) We can add together all changes in inventories. (2) We can cancel the purchases of raw materials from the sales of raw materials, since they both appear on the left-hand side of the statement, once with a plus sign and once with a minus sign. For example, the purchases of raw materials by the consumer-goods firm exactly cancels the sales to the consumer-goods firm by the raw-materials firm. (3) We can add together the purchases of buildings and equipment by the consumer-goods firm and the raw-materials firm (sales of buildings and equipment by the capital-goods firm) and the buildings and equipment that the capital-goods firm has manufactured for itself. We shall call the sum of these items "purchases of buildings and equipment." (4) On the right-hand side, we can add together all wages and salaries paid by all of the firms and label it "wages and salaries." All of the other items on this side can be treated in the same way. The GBP statement then appears as shown in Table 2-4.

Table 2-4. Gross-Business Product Statement

Sales to consumers	$115	Wages and salaries	$107
Changes in inventories	7	Rent	7
Purchases of buildings and equipment	36	Interest	10
		Depreciation	20
		Profits	14
Gross national product	$158	Gross national product	$158

Although we have imagined that there are only three firms, whereas in reality there are millions in our economy, the example illustrates all of the conceptional problems involved in finding the gross business product from information for individual firms. Whether there is one firm or a thousand firms, the GBP is the sum of the values added by all firms. When there is only one firm, the GBP statement is the same as its value-added statement which, in turn, is the same as its production statement. When there are many firms, however, we must establish a value-added statement for each firm, and sum up the numbers found there. The value added by a firm is not likely to be the same as its production; since most firms buy products from other firms, the value-added statements and the production statements will not be the same.

QUESTIONS

1. Although purchases of raw materials appear on the left-hand side of the value-added statement, and the GBP statement is the sum of the value-added statements, they do not appear in the final GBP statement. Why not?
2. It is generally assumed that the product created in households is equal to the wages and salaries paid by the households. Assuming that households paid $200 in wages and salaries, prepare a value-

added statement for households. (*Hint.* Think of servants as businesses who sell their services to households for wages and salaries. But do not list their income as profits; list it as wages and salaries.)

IV. INVESTMENT

A country's capital stock is the total value of all of its inventories, buildings, and equipment. Gross private domestic investment (GPDI), during a period, is the sum of all additions to buildings and equipment and changes in inventories; it is the gross change in the capital stock. If at the beginning of a year a society had \$50 worth of buildings, \$40 worth of equipment, and \$25 worth of inventories, its capital stock was \$115 (that is, \$50 + \$40 + \$25). If, during the year, new buildings worth \$10 were constructed, new equipment worth \$5 was constructed, and inventories fell by \$2, GPDI would have been \$13 (that is, \$10 + \$5 − \$2).

Be careful to note what has and has not been included in the capital stock. It includes buildings, equipment, and inventories, and nothing else. It does not include money, stocks, or bonds. The term has been given a technical definition that does not correspond fully to its everyday usage. When someone says that John Smith has lots of capital, it may mean that he has lots of money or lots of securities. We are not, however, using the term that way. A person, as far as we are concerned, has capital if he holds inventories, or if he owns buildings or equipment. Your capital increases, you invest, only when you add to inventories, buildings, or equipment.

GPDI and net private domestic investment (NPDI) must be carefully distinguished. If you know the capital stock at the beginning of the year and if you know GPDI, you would *not* know the capital stock at the end of the period. Although you know what you started with and you know what has been added, you do not know what has been subtracted. In order to find the new capital stock you must also know depreciation.

NPDI differs from GPDI by depreciation. If GPDI is \$13 and depreciation is \$3, then NPDI is \$10. NPDI is the *net* addition to the capital stock; it is the sum of all of the additions to buildings and equipment *minus* depreciation, plus changes in inventories. Given a knowledge of the capital stock at the beginning of the year and NPDI, you know the capital stock at the end of the period. If the capital stock at the beginning was $115 and NPDI was $10, then the capital stock at the end is $125.

In the gross business product statement (Table 2-4), changes in inventories and purchases of buildings and equipment are found on the left. If these two items are added together, GPDI is found. It is $43. The GBP can, therefore, be reported as shown in Table 2-5.

Table 2-5. Statement of Gross Product Created Within Business Sector in Absence of Government and Foreign Trade

Sales to consumers (C)	$115	Wages and salaries	$107
Gross private domestic investment (GPDI)	43	Rent	7
		Interest	10
		Depreciation	20
		Profits	14
Gross business product	$158	Gross business product	$158

QUESTIONS

1. The people in an economy have $50 worth of money, $75 worth of inventories, $100 worth of common stocks, $60 worth of bonds, $100 worth of buildings, and $85 worth of equipment. Explain why the capital stock is $260 rather than $470.
2. Given the following information, compute NPDI for 1966:

	January 1, 1966	*December 31, 1966*
Inventories	$ 400	$ 350
Buildings	250	275
Equipment	175	225

If depreciation during 1966 was 40, what was GPDI?

V. NET NATIONAL-PRODUCT STATEMENT

If we not only abstract from the existence of government and foreign trade, but assume that no product is created within households, the GBP is equal to the GNP. The GNP statement is then the same as the GBP statement. We learned in the previous chapter that the NNP differs from the GNP by depreciation. If depreciation is subtracted from both sides of the GBP statement, a net-national-product statement is obtained (Table 2-6). The left-hand side consists of sales to consumers plus GPDI minus depreciation. Since NPDI is GPDI minus depreciation, the left-hand side then is simply sales to consumers plus NPDI.

Table 2-6. Statement of Net National Product in Absence of Government, Foreign Trade, and Production within Households

Sales to consumers	$115	Wages and salaries	$107
Net private domestic investment (NPDI)	23	Rents	7
		Interest	10
		Profits	14
Net national product	$138	National income	$138

VI. SAVING

Saving is the part of income that is not consumed. If you have an income of $5000 and if you spend $3000 on consumer goods and services, then, by definition, you have saved $2000.

Nothing in this definition implies that you must hold money when you save; saving is not necessarily hoarding. Your $2000 worth of saving may be used to buy bonds or stocks; it may be lent to a friend or relative; it may be put into a bank; or it may be put under your mattress. But, in any case, you have saved, because you have failed to spend all of your income on consumer goods and services.

QUESTIONS

1. Assume that during a period of time some individual has received an income of $4000. Assuming that he also conducted the following transactions during that same period of time, how much of his income did he save?

   Sold $21,000 worth of utility stocks.
   Bought $18,000 worth of government bonds.
   Put $3000 into his savings account.
   Bought $3500 worth of consumer goods and services.
   Secured a $40,000 mortgage from a bank.
   With the mortgage money and $10,000 that he had in his checking account, he bought a house for $50,000.

VII. THE EQUALITY OF SAVING AND INVESTMENT

The net-national-product-and-national-income statement (Table 2-6) records a national income of $138 with sales to consumers of $115. Net private savings (NPS), therefore, was $23 (that is $138 − $115), since saving is defined as the difference between income and consumption. Gross private saving is NPS plus depreciation.

But not only is NPS equal to $23, so is NPDI. This is no accident. NPS, as defined, is necessarily equal to NPDI; it cannot be anything else. If sales to consumers are subtracted from the NNP on the left side of net-national-product-and-national-income statement, NPDI remains. If sales to consumers is subtracted from the national income, which is necessarily equal to the NNP, NPS remains. Thus net private saving must equal net private domestic investment.

To make certain that you understand this equality and to convince you that it is nothing but an accounting identity (something that must be true by definition), consider the following hypothetical actions—actions that one might think would affect saving differently from investment.

A. *Someone Has a Haircut and Pays the Barber $1.75*

The person who has had the haircut has used $1.75 of his income and, therefore, has reduced his saving by $1.75. The transaction does not affect the amount of buildings, equipment, or inventories; investment would be unchanged. Does not that mean that saving is down $1.75 without investment changing, so that they would be unequal? The answer must be no. The trick in this case is to realize that since investment in the community has not changed, saving also has not changed. The person who paid for the haircut has saved $1.75 less, but the barber has the $1.75. His income is up $1.75, and since he has not consumed it—he has not had a chance to—the barber has saved $1.75 more. Total saving is also unchanged.

B. *Someone Buys a Tube of Toothpaste for 89¢*

The buyer's saving is down 89¢, since he has increased his consumption by that amount. Now consider the store that has sold the toothpaste. If the retailer paid 89¢ for the toothpaste, his inventories would be down by that amount. Since inventories are part of capital stock, a reduction in inventories means that NPDI has been reduced. In this case, therefore, NPS and NPDI are both reduced by 89¢.

It would be more realistic to assume, however, that the retailer paid less than 89¢ for the toothpaste. If the toothpaste cost the retailer 45¢, his inventories would only be down that amount. Saving appears to be down 89¢, but NPDI is down only 45¢. Would saving and investment no longer be equal? Of course, the answer must be no. NPDI is reduced by 45¢ and saving must be also. The trick here is to realize that the retailer has made a profit of 44¢; he has earned that much income. Since he has not yet spent that income buying consumer goods, he has saved 44¢ more. The person who bought the toothpaste saved 89¢ less, while the retailer saved 44¢ more. NPS is, therefore, down by the difference, 45¢, the same amount as NPDI.

C. *A Manufacturer Spends $50 on Raw Materials*

He has invested $50 more, since he has increased his inventories by that amount. But the seller of the raw materials has reduced his inventories as a result of the sale. If the materials cost him $50 to manufacture, he has reduced his investment by the same amount that the buyer has increased his. Neither NPS nor NPDI is changed. If, on the other hand, the raw materials cost less than $50 to manufacture, for example $35, then the seller of the raw materials had reduced his inventories by $35 and earned $15 worth of income, which he has saved, since we have not given him a chance to spend it yet. NPS is up $15. The buyer has invested $50 more, while the seller has invested $35 less; therefore, NPDI is up $15, exactly the same amount as saving.

D. *The Manufacturer Hires Labor to Work on the Raw Materials and Pays the Labor $20*

The raw materials were worth $50, but with the labor expended on them, valued at cost, they are now worth $70. Therefore, the manufacturer's investment is up $20. Labor has received $20 in income, and has not yet spent it; saving is also up $20.

QUESTIONS

1. In each instance below, indicate by exactly how much NPS and NPDI are changed.
   (a) You go to the movie, paying $0.75.
   (b) A manufacturer sells inventories, which cost him $50, to a wholesaler for $60.
   (c) You buy a cotton shirt for $5.50 from a retailer who paid $3.00 for it, and who gives his clerks a 10% commission.
   (d) A manufacturer pays $100 in wages for labor for working on goods that still have to be sold.

VIII. IF NPS EQUALS NPDI, DOES SPENDING EQUAL OUTPUT?

We argued in the previous chapter that saving did not necessarily lead to spending on capital, but we have just learned that saving is always equal to investment. Is there a contradiction implied here, or are these two statements compatible?

They are compatible; there is no contradiction. It is true that saving necessarily equals investment, but it does not follow that savers spend on capital or lend to others who spend on capital all that they have saved. If an output of $100 is produced and only $80 is spent on consumer goods, saving would be $20. As a consequence, someone must be holding the $20 worth of output that has not been sold to consumers; someone has more buildings, equipment, or inventories. The goods may be in the hands of producers, wholesalers, or retailers. Whether they wanted to or not, they invested $20.

Saving equals investment; they are both $20. But investment may be *undesired*, and the economy may be in trouble. If producers discover that they cannot sell all that they have produced, they will cut back their production and unemployment will occur. Saving leads to investment, but if spending on capital is not equal to saving, then the investment is unwanted. Output will fall and unemployment occur.

Let us not be fooled, therefore, into thinking that the necessary equality between NPS and NPDI implies that spending is necessarily equal to output. Only if investors wish to spend $20 on inventories, buildings, or equipment would total spending be equal to the NNP. Only if the *desire to invest* equals saving would there be no deficiency of demand.

QUESTIONS

1. "Imagine that the NNP is $200 and that consumers spend $150 and hoard their savings. Since saving is necessarily equal to investment, we know that someone is holding the goods that have not been sold to consumers. They clearly demand the goods that consumers do not buy; they demand $50 worth of goods. When their demand is added to consumer demand, we see that total demand is exactly equal to total output. All that is produced is demanded; a glut of goods is impossible." Why do you not agree?

IX. THE RELATIONSHIP OF EMPLOYMENT TO NNP

We are in the process of developing a theory of output, based on the assumption that wages and prices are inflexible *downward*. Imagine that under these circumstances, nonfrictional, involuntary unemployment exists; more people are looking for work than there are jobs available. If output is to increase this month, more labor is needed to produce the increased output. There is a relationship between employment and output. If output goes up, so does employment. If output goes down, employment goes down. In the section that follows we shall develop an elementary, Keynesian theory of output but, because of the relationship between output and employment, our theory of output will also be a theory of employment.

X. THE AGGREGATE SUPPLY FUNCTION

Given fixed prices and wages, business firms are willing to produce all they can sell. If demand rises, firms will try to expand their production by hiring more labor. If there is unemployed labor, they will experience no difficulty finding more workers. Demand, then, is the determinant of production. The relationship between output and the demand for output is precise. So long as unemployment exists, equilibrium output will equal the demand for output. If less is being produced than demanded, profits can be increased by expanding production. If more is being produced than demanded, profits are endangered as unsold goods pile up, so production is cut. Only when output equals the demand for output can there be equilibrium.

Assuming that the NNP at full employment (NNP_f) is equal to 200, the relationship between output and the demand for output is shown in Table 2-7.

Table 2-7.

If Aggregate Demand for Output is:	In Equilibrium NNP Will Be:
0	0
10	10
20	20
30	30
—	—
180	180
190	190
200	$200 = NNP_f$
210	$200 = NNP_f$
220	$200 = NNP_f$

The relationship between aggregate supply and demand contained in Table 2-7 is depicted in Figure 2-1. Aggregate demand for output is placed on the vertical axis and NNP on the horizontal. Output (NNP) is shown to be equal to the aggregate demand for output until they equal 200. Beyond that point, NNP is 200 no matter how great aggregate demand. Until full employment is reached, the slope of the line is unity; at full employment the curve becomes vertical.

QUESTIONS

1. Why could not the following equations be the aggregate supply function?

   (a) Aggregate supply = 2 times aggregate demand
   (b) Aggregate supply = $\frac{1}{2}$ aggregate demand

2. If NNP_f is 200, what would equilibrium NNP be if aggregate demand were 250?

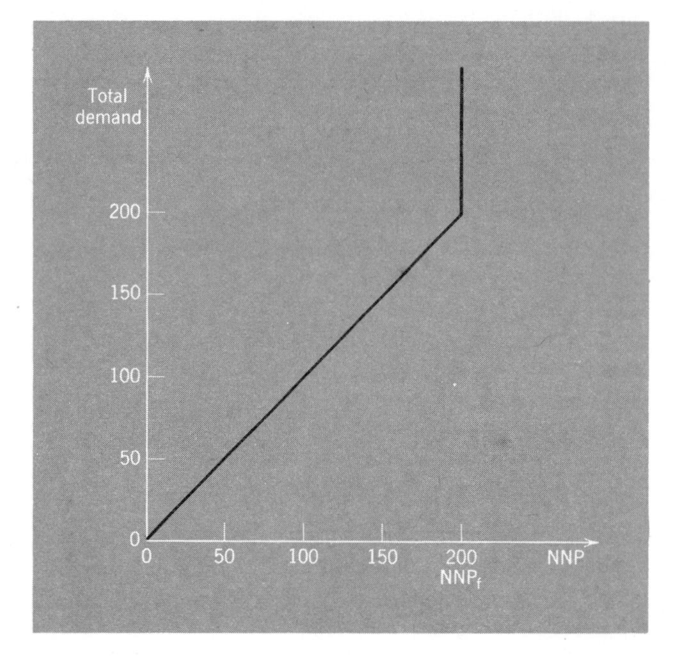

Figure 2-1

XI. THE AGGREGATE DEMAND FOR OUTPUT

Since output is determined by the demand for output, in order to explain output and employment we must explain the demand for output. What determines the aggregate demand for output?

Continuing to assume that there is no government or foreign trade, aggregate demand for output can be broken into two components: consumption demand (the demand of households for consumer goods and services) and investment demand (the demand, net of depreciation, for new buildings and equipment plus additions to inventories). To explain aggregate demand, we must explain what determines consumption and investment demand. Let us consider consumption demand first.

XII. CONSUMPTION DEMAND

How much the community will spend on consumer goods and services depends on many, many things. But total consumption expenditures in any period is most importantly affected by income (NNP). The more income an individual has, the more he buys, and the better he lives. The more income the community has, the more it spends on consumer goods and services.

Table 2-8 records a hypothetical relationship between consumption demand, savings, and national income (NNP).

Table 2-8.

If NNP is:	Consumption Would be:	Saving Would be:
0	20	–20
20	36	–16
40	52	–12
60	68	– 8
80	84	– 4
100	100	0
120	116	4
140	132	8
160	148	12
180	164	16
200	180	20

The relationship between consumption demand and NNP has three important characteristics.

First, when income increases consumption increases, but by less than the increase in income. The change in consumption demand divided by the change in income is defined as the *marginal propensity to consume.* In our example, the marginal propensity to consume is 0.8. When income increases from zero to 20, consumption demand increases from 20 to 36. The change in consumption is 16, and the change in income is 20. The ratio of the change in consumption to the change in income is 0.8 [that is, (36–20)/(20–0)]. In this example, the marginal propensity to consume is always 0.8. Although the marginal propensity to consume may be other than 0.8 and may not be the same at all income levels—when income is small it may be greater than when income is high—it is always less than 1. The first law of consumption demand then states: *the marginal propensity to consume is a positive fraction.*

Second, when income increases, the ratio of consumption demand to income decreases. Consumption demand divided by NNP is defined as *the average propensity to consume.* When income is 20, consumption demand is 36; the average propensity to consume is then 1.6; (36/20). When income is 100, the average propensity to consume is 1, and when income is 200 the average propensity to consume is 0.9. The second law of consumption demand then states: *the average propensity to consume decreases as income increases.*

Finally, our Table 2-8 indicates that if income were zero, consumption would be greater than zero; when NNP equals zero, consumption would be 20. In general, at low levels of income, consumption would be greater than income; the average propensity to consume would be greater than 1. The third law of consumption demand then states: *the average propensity to consume is greater than 1 at low levels of income.*

If we know NNP and consumption, we know saving as well, since it is defined as the difference between NNP and consumption. In column 3 of Table 2-8 saving is given. It was found by subtracting the number in the second column (consumption) from the number in the first column (NNP).

There are three laws of saving, corresponding to and implied by the three laws of consumption.

First, as income increases, saving increases but by less than income. The change in saving divided by the change in income is defined to be *the marginal propensity to save.* In our example, the marginal propensity to save is 0.2. When income increases from 0 to 20, saving increases from −20 to −16. The change in saving is 4 and the change in income is 20. The ratio of the change in saving to the change in income is 0.2 [that is, (−16 − −20)/(20 − 0)]. In our tables the marginal propensity to save is always 0.2. Although the marginal propensity to save may be other than 0.2 and need not be the same at all income levels—when income is small it may be less than when income in high—it is always less than 1. The first law of saving then states: *the marginal propensity to save is a positive fraction.*

Second, when income increases, the ratio of saving to income increases. Saving divided by NNP is defined as *the average propensity to save.* When income is 20, saving is −16; the average propensity to save is -0.8 (that is, $-16/20$). When income is 100, the average propensity to save is zero, and when income is 200 the average propensity to save is 0.2. The second law of saving then states: *the average propensity to save increases as income increases.*

Finally, if income were zero, saving would be negative. In our example, when income is zero, saving is -20. This is merely another way of stating that at low levels of income, saving would be negative; the average propensity to save would be less than zero. The third law of saving, then, states: *the average propensity to save is negative at low levels of income.*

The information about NNP, consumption demand, and saving shown in Table 2-8 is also depicted in Figure 2-2. This diagram shows consumption demand as a function of income in the upper portion and saving as a function of income in the lower. The slopes of the curves are the marginal propensities to consume and to save. The slope of the upper line is 0.8 (the marginal propensity to consume), while the slope of the lower line is 0.2 (the marginal propensity to save).

The marginal propensity to save is equal to 1 minus the marginal propensity to consume. In our example, the marginal propensity to consume is 0.8, and, therefore, the marginal propensity to save is 0.2. The reason for this relationship is clear. Since saving is defined as the difference between income and consumption, if you consume x tenths of an increase in income, you must save $1 - x$ tenths of the increase.

QUESTIONS

1. Draw a consumption function (consumption demand on the vertical axis and NNP on the horizontal) so that the average propensity to consume is always equal to the marginal propensity to consume and so that both are constant.
2. Reproduce the consumption function shown in Figure 2-2. Now reduce the marginal propensity to consume without changing the average propensity to consume at the point at which NNP equals 100.
3. Draw a consumption function so that consumption demand would be 10 if NNP were zero and so that the marginal propensity to consume is 0.75.

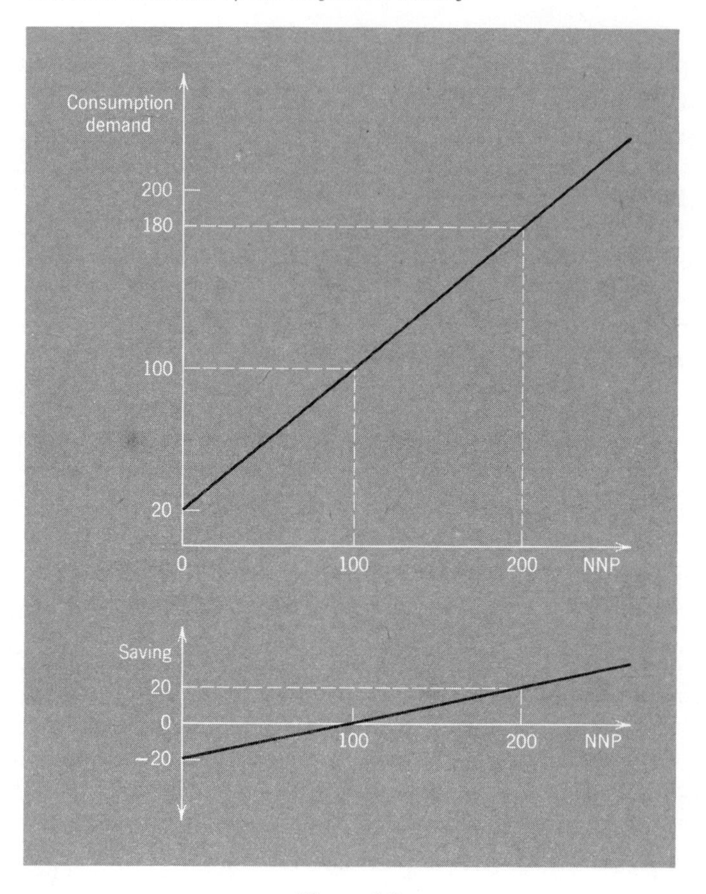

Figure 2-2

4. Draw the saving function that corresponds to the consumption function in Question 3.
5. Why is the sum of the average propensity to consume and average propensity to save necessarily equal to 1?

XIII. EQUILIBRIUM NNP WHEN INVESTMENT DEMAND IS ZERO

Imagine, for the moment, that there is no desire to invest; investment demand is zero. What would national income (NNP) be in equilibrium? Would full employment be possible? Since full-employment NNP (NNP_f) is 200, there will only be jobs for all if total demand is also 200. But with government expenditures, exports, and investment demand all assumed to be equal to zero, the only demand for output would be consumption demand, and it is not 200 when NNP is 200; It is only 180. If business firms produced a total output of 200, spending on consumer goods and services would be 180; 20 would be saved. But if 20 is saved, we know that NPDI would also be 20, since saving is necessarily equal to investment. Businesses would discover that they were unable to sell all that they produced; they would have 20 in unsold goods in their inventories. This *undesired* investment would produce a reaction. In order to get rid of their unwanted inventories and bring production into line with demand, producers would lay-off workers and reduce their output. If output was at the full-employment level, to begin with, it would not remain there.

Table 2-8 indicates that, for any level of NNP greater than 100, consumption demand would be *less* than NNP. At income levels greater than 100, therefore, producers would be unable to sell everything produced, and output and employment would fall.

It is equally clear that at all levels of NNP less than 100, consumption demand would be *greater* than NNP. For all income levels less than 100, therefore, producers would be able to sell more than the entire production, and output and employment would rise.

Equilibrium NNP is, therefore, 100. Only at this level of NNP will aggregate demand exactly equal NNP; only at this level will producers be able to sell just the amount that they produce.

The consumption demand line in Figure 2-2 and the supply curve for aggregate output in Figure 2-1 are both shown in Figure 2-3. Since we are, at present, assuming that the only demand for output is consumption demand, consumption demand and the aggregate demand for output are the same thing, and both can be shown on the vertical axis.

Equilibrium output (NNP_e) is found at the point where the supply curve and the aggregate demand curve intersect; it is 100. At any other level of NNP, aggregate demand is either greater or less than NNP; producers are able to sell more than they produced or cannot sell all that they have produced. If NNP

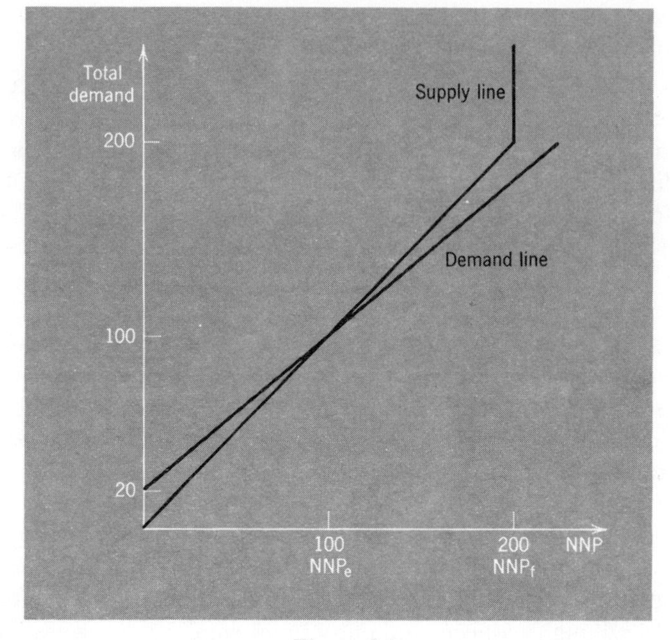

Figure 2-3

were 50, for example, aggregate demand (consumption) would be 60. If NNP were 150, for example, aggregate demand would be 140.

Equilibrium output can also be found from the saving line in Figure 2-2. Equilibrium requires that

$$NNP = \text{aggregate demand.}$$

In the example under consideration, aggregate demand consists only of consumption demand. Therefore,

$$NNP = \text{consumption demand.}$$

Since NNP and national income are identical and saving is defined as the difference between national income and consumption,

$$\text{Saving} + \text{consumption} = NNP.$$

It, therefore, follows that

$$\text{Saving} = 0.$$

Equilibrium NNP (NNP_e) is found in Figure 2-2 at 100, where saving is zero.

If NNP were less than 100, saving would be negative. Since NPS is necessarily equal to NPDI, investment would also be negative. But we are assuming that business firms wish neither to invest nor disinvest, neither add to their capital nor subtract from it. If consumers are able to buy all the goods that they are demanding, producers would be forced to give up inventories, which they do not wish to lose. In order to re-establish their inventories and bring production into line with demand, they would hire more labor and expand output.

If NNP were greater than 100, saving would be positive. Since NPS is necessarily equal to NPDI, investment would also be positive. But we are assuming that business firms wish neither to invest nor disinvest, neither add to their capital nor subtract from it. If consumers saved, producers would be forced to add to their inventories when they do not wish to do so. In order to rid themselves of unwanted inventories and to bring production into line with demand, they would lay-off workers and contract output.

QUESTIONS

1. Why would NNP_e equal total consumption demand in equilibrium, if investment demand, government expenditures, and exports were all zero?
2. Assuming that consumption demand would be 10 if NNP were zero and that the marginal propensity to consume is 0.5, what would NNP_e be if the only demand for goods was consumption demand?
3. If the marginal and average propensities to consume were constant and equal and if consumption demand were the only demand, what would NNP_e be?
4. How is it possible that NPDI can be positive while investment demand is zero?
5. What would happen if NPDI were positive and investment demand were zero?

XIV. EQUILIBRIUM NNP WITH POSITIVE INVESTMENT DEMAND

In the following chapter we shall discuss the determinants of investment demand. For now, let us assume that investment demand is some given amount, for instance, 10. If this is the case, what would equilibrium national income be?

Table 2-9 contains the same information as Table 2-8 plus the new assumption that investment demand is 10. Equilibrium NNP is no longer 100; it is 150, since only at that level of NNP is aggregate demand (the sum of consumption demand plus investment demand) exactly equal to NNP. For all income levels less than 150, aggregate demand is greater than NNP, while for all income levels greater than 150 aggregate demand is less.

Table 2-9.

If NNP is:	Consumption Would Be:	Investment Demand Would Be:	Aggregate Demand Would Be:	Saving Would Be:	NNP Would
0	20	10	30	—20	Increase
20	36	10	46	—16	Increase
40	52	10	62	—12	Increase
60	68	10	78	— 8	Increase
80	84	10	94	— 4	Increase
100	100	10	110	0	Increase
120	116	10	126	4	Increase
140	132	10	142	8	Increase
150	140	10	150	10	No change
160	148	10	158	12	Decrease
180	164	10	174	16	Decrease
200	180	10	190	20	Decrease

In Figure 2-4, equilibrium national income is found at the intersection of the aggregate demand curve and the supply curve, as it was in Figure 2-3. The only difference is that investment demand has been added to consumption demand. The total demand line has been moved upward by 10.

At the intersection of the supply and demand curves, NNP is 150. Equilibrium income is, therefore, this amount. If NNP were greater than 150, you can see that the aggregate demand for output would be less than NNP. Producers would be unable to sell all they produced, and would lay-off workers and cut back production. If NNP were less than 150, aggregate demand would exceed NNP; workers would be hired and production increased.

An inspection of Table 2-9 will indicate that at equilibrium

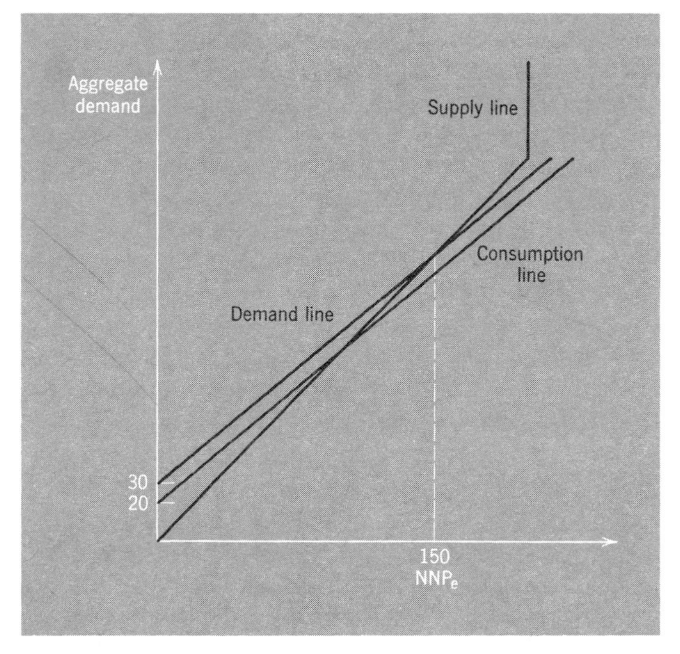

Figure 2-4

NNP saving is equal to investment demand. Can we conclude that saving is always equal to investment demand in equilibrium?

We know that the aggregate demand for output equals consumption demand plus investment demand. Since saving is the difference between income (NNP) and consumption, we also know that NNP equals consumption plus saving. Since NNP equals consumption plus investment demand and also consumption plus saving, consumption plus investment demand is equal to consumption plus saving. But if this is the case, investment demand is equal to saving. It is, therefore, true that investment demand is always equal to saving in equilibrium.

Figure 2-5 contains the saving curve and an investment curve. The saving curve is exactly the same as in Figure 2-2. The investment demand curve is drawn as a horizontal line at the level of 10, since we are assuming that investment demand is always 10. Equilibrium NNP is found at the point at which investment demand is equal to saving; it is 150.

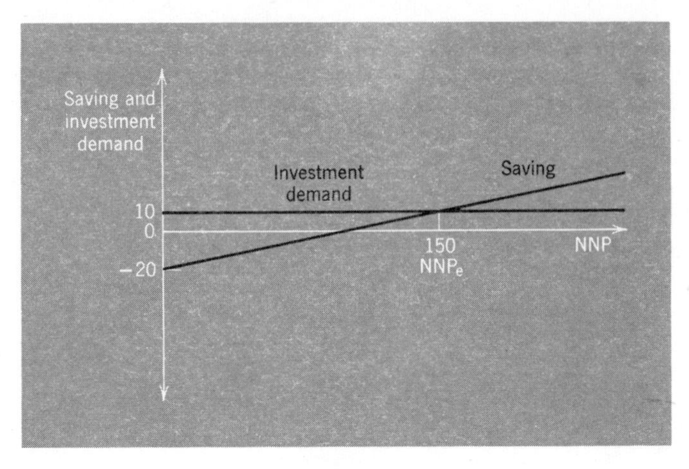

Figure 2-5

QUESTIONS

1. If investment demand were 25, if consumption demand were 20 when NNP is zero, and if the marginal propensity to consume were 0.9, what would equilibrium NNP be?
2. Verify your answer to Question 1 with an aggregate demand and NNP diagram. Use the graph on the next page.
3. Verify your answer to Question 1 with a saving and investment-demand diagram. Use the graph on the next page.
4. Explain how it is possible that NPDI could be 40 when investment demand is only 20.
5. If NNP is 500, if consumption demand is 400, and if investment demand is 200:
   (a) What would saving be?
   (b) What would NPDI be?
   (c) Would NNP tend to increase or decrease?

XV. DO NOT CONFUSE AN IDENTITY WITH AN EQUILIBRIUM CONDITION

This is a good point at which to warn against confusing two statements. One is that saving is equal to investment, and the other is that saving is equal to investment demand. The first is an accounting identity, something that must always be true. The second is

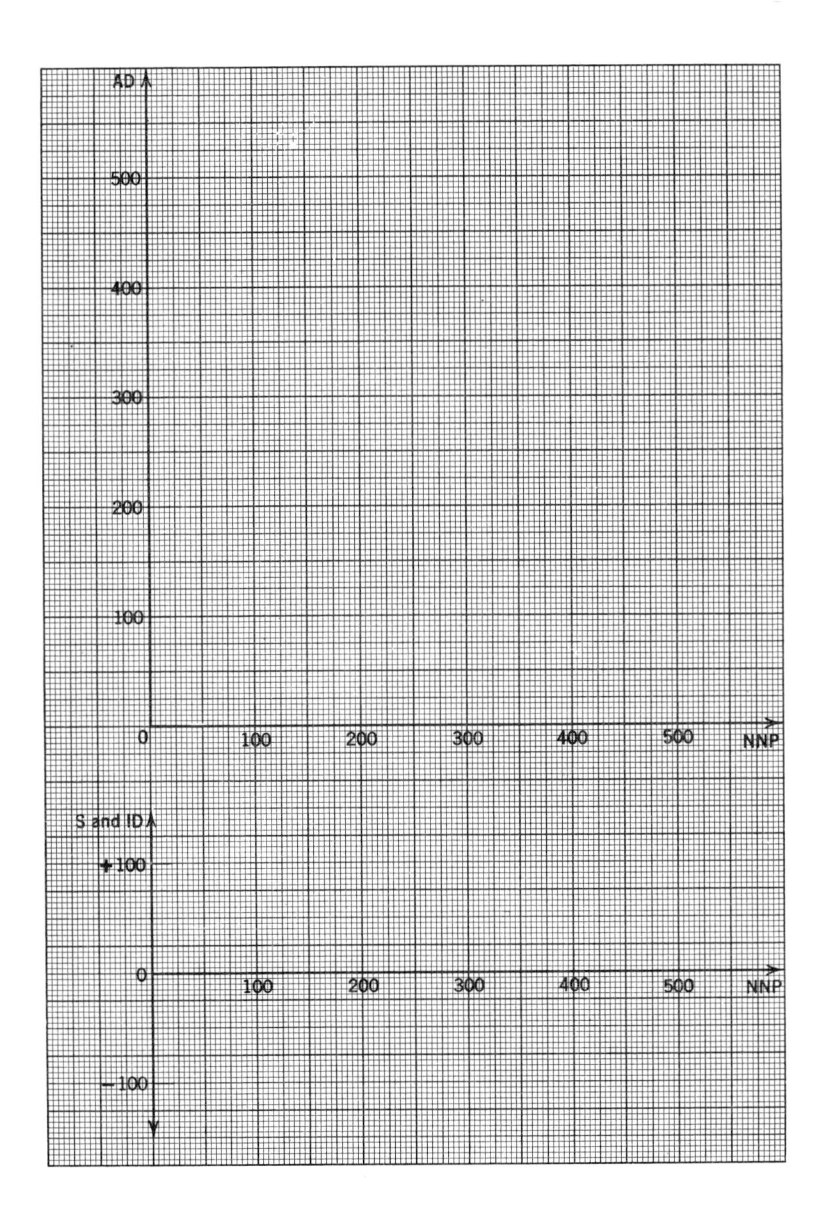

AD
500
400
300
200
100
0
100
200
300
400
500
NNP
S and ID
+100
0
100
200
300
400
500
NNP
−100

an equilibrium condition; it need not be true, but is true when there is no tendency for change.

In the example in Figure 2-5, we know that output cannot be 200 in equilibrium, since at that output saving is greater than investment demand. When saving is greater than investment demand, saving plus consumption is greater than investment demand plus consumption demand. But saving plus consumption is NNP, while investment demand plus consumption demand is total demand. To state that saving is greater than investment demand is equivalent to stating that NNP is greater than aggregate demand. We know when this occurs; firms are unable to sell all they are producing, and then they lay-off workers and reduce production.

Although saving would exceed *investment demand* at an output of 200, saving would equal *Investment* at that output. If output were 200, saving would be 20. If consumers save 20 of their income they spend 180 of consumer goods and services. But if an output of 200 is produced and 180 of that is consumed, producers, wholesalers, or retailers must be holding the rest of the output; they must have invested 20.

One way of explaining why equilibrium output could not be 200 in equilibrium is to say that at that output business wishes to invest 10, but is actually investing 20. Since business firms are adding to buildings, equipment, and inventories more than they wish to add, they contract production and NNP falls.

XVI. THE INVESTMENT AND CONSUMPTION MULTIPLIERS

When we assumed that there was no investment demand we discovered that equilibrium NNP would be 100. When we assumed that investment demand was 10, we found that equilibrium NNP would be 150. It appears, therefore, that an increase in investment demand of 10 results in an increase in equilibrium NNP of 50; each dollar of investment demand generates $50 worth of income.

If the marginal propensity to consume is a positive fraction, as we are assuming, then a change in investment demand will always lead to a multiple change in equilibrium NNP. The change in NNP divided by the change in investment demand is the *investment multiplier.*

The multiplier depends on the marginal propensity to consume. To be precise: the change in equilibrium NNP will be equal to the change in investment demand multiplied by the reciprocal of 1 minus the marginal propensity to consume. In our example the marginal propensity to consume was 0.8. One minus the marginal propensity to consume is 0.2. The reciprocal of 0.2 is 5 (0.2 divided into 1 is 5); the investment multiplier is 5.

Proof of this proposition can easily be derived from Figure 2-5. When investment demand was zero, equilibrium NNP was 100; it was found at the point where saving was also zero. When investment demand was 10, equilibrium NNP was 150; it was found at the point where saving was equal to investment demand. Now the investment multiplier is the change in income divided by the change in investment demand. Since the change is income was 50 and the change in investment demand was 10, the multiplier was 5. Five is exactly the same as the reciprocal of 0.2, but 0.2 is the slope of the saving curve in Figure 2-5. Therefore, we can conclude that the multiplier is the reciprocal of the marginal propensity to save. We also know, however, that the marginal propensity to save is equal to 1 minus the marginal propensity to consume. It, therefore, follows that the multiplier is also equal to the reciprocal of 1 minus the marginal propensity to consume.

If consumption demand were to increase at every income level, it would also result in a multiple increase in NNP, and the consumption multiplier is the same as the investment multiplier. Assume, for example, that the relationship between consumption and NNP that is found in Table 2-9 is altered so that at every income level consumption demand would be 10 greater. Previously we found that with investment demand equal to zero, equilibrium NNP would be 100. But what would equilibrium NNP be, with zero investment demand, if consumption demand were 10 greater at each income level? We must find the level of NNP at which NNP is equal to consumption demand. If NNP were 100, aggregate demand would be 110; this could not be equilibrium. If NNP were 120, aggregate demand would be 126; this could not be equilibrium. Only at an NNP of 150 would aggregate demand equal NNP, since at that level of income aggregate demand would also be 150.

We can also derive this result from an examination of Figures

2-4 and 2-5. Aggregate demand (the sum of consumption demand and investment demand is measured as the vertical axis in Figure 2-4. If the aggregate curve is shifted upward by 10, equilibrium NNP will rise by 50. It makes no difference why the aggregate demand curve is increased. Investment demand could have risen by 10 or consumption demand could have increased at each income level by 10. Clearly, then, a change in investment demand and a change in consumption at each income level will have the same effect on equilibrium NNP. The investment multiplier and the consumption multiplier are the same.

If consumption increases at each income level by 10, then saving decreases at each income level by that amount. On a saving-and-investment demand graph such as Figure 2-5, you would show an increase in consumption demand at every income level of 10 by lowering the saving curve at each income level by 10. If the saving curve intersected the vertical axis at −20 previously, it would now intersect at −30. Such a change in the saving curve would have exactly the same effect on equilibrium NNP as an increase in the investment demand curve by 10.

The multiplier, whether investment or consumption, is not a complicated idea. It all comes about because consumption depends on income. If investment demand rises by 10, business firms will produce that much more output in order to satisfy all the demand. But if output rises by 10, so does income, since they are necessarily equal. But a rise in income leads to an increase in consumption demand. With more consumer goods and services being demanded, business firms will expand output still further. This further expansion of output and income leads to a further expansion of consumption demand which, in turn, will lead business to hire still more labor in order to expand output still further. And so it goes. The multiplier just tells what the total effect will be.

QUESTIONS

1. If consumption demand were equal to exactly 0.99999999999 times NNP and if it were the only demand for output, what would NNP be in equilibrium? If investment demand were $1, what would NNP_e be?

2. If consumption demand became 5 greater at each level of NNP, exactly what would happen to the saving line?
3. What is wrong with the following statement?
   "If, at the equilibrium income level, the average propensity to consume were unchanged while the marginal propensity to consume increased, NNP_e would increase." (*Hint.* Draw an aggregate-demand-and-aggregate-supply-diagram.)
4. If the investment multiplier is 10, what is the marginal propensity to save?

XVII. AN ALGEBRAIC GENERALIZATION OF THE MULTIPLIERS

We have developed an analysis by assuming a specific relationship between consumption demand and NNP and by assuming specific values for investment demand, either zero or 10. Let us now generalize the analysis.

Assume that consumption demand would be positive even if NNP were zero. Consumption demand (*CD*) at the zero level of income can be called autonomous consumption (*AC*), since it is not determined by NNP. Assume, further, that the marginal propensity to consume (*mpc*) is constant. Given these assumptions, we have the following relationship between consumption demand and NNP.

$$CD = AC + mpcNNP. \tag{2.1}$$

Aggregate demand (*AD*) consists of consumption demand plus investment demand (*ID*). Therefore,

$$AD = CD + ID. \tag{2.2}$$

Finally, *NNP* is equal to *AD*, so long as *AD* is less than NNP_f.

$$NNP = AD \tag{2.3}$$

If Eq. 2.1 is substituted into Eq. 2.2, and then Eq. 2.2 is substituted into Eq. 2.3, we have

$$NNP = AC + mpcNNP + ID. \tag{2.4}$$

If *mpcNNP* is brought to the left-hand side and NNP factored out of the expression, we have

$$(1 - mpc)\ NNP = AC + ID. \tag{2.5}$$

Dividing through by $(1 - mpc)$ and writing the result in a convenient form, we have

$$NNP = \frac{1}{1 - mpc} AC + \frac{1}{1 - mpc} ID. \qquad (2.6)$$

Since we are assuming that the *mpc* is constant, we can rewrite this expression as

$$\Delta NNP = \frac{1}{1 - mpc} \Delta AC + \frac{1}{1 - mpc} \Delta ID, \qquad (2.7)$$

where Δ is the symbol for a small change. If ID changes without any change in AC (ΔAC is zero), we have

$$\frac{\Delta NNP}{\Delta ID} = \frac{1}{1 - mpc}. \qquad (2.8)$$

If AC changes without any change in ID (ΔID is zero), we have

$$\frac{\Delta NNP}{\Delta AC} = \frac{1}{1 - mpc}. \qquad (2.9)$$

Equations 2.8 and 2.9 are the investment and consumption multipliers; they are both equal to the reciprocal of one minus the marginal propensity to consume.

Since NNP is equal to consumption demand plus saving, we have then

$$\Delta NNP = \Delta CD + \Delta S. \qquad (2.10)$$

Dividing both sides of Eq. 2.10 by ΔNNP, we find

$$1 - \frac{\Delta CD}{\Delta NNP} = \frac{\Delta S}{\Delta NNP}. \qquad (2.11)$$

But $\Delta CD/\Delta NNP$ is the marginal propensity to consume and $\Delta S/\Delta NNP$ is the marginal propensity to save (*mps*). Therefore, Equations 2.8 and 2.9 can be rewritten as

$$\frac{\Delta NNP}{\Delta ID} = \frac{1}{mps} \qquad (2.12)$$

and

$$\frac{\Delta NNP}{\Delta AC} = \frac{1}{mps}. \qquad (2.13)$$

XVIII. CONCLUSIONS

In the previous chapter we examined the classical argument that aggregate demand always equals NNP. We found this view to be indefensible. The theory presented in the present chapter implies that the aggregate demand for output need not equal output. Only when the desire to consume and the desire to invest are sufficiently great will output be at its full-employment level and will there be jobs for all.

In the chapters that follow we shall pursue the analysis further, and indicate what actions the government can take to correct a situation in which the aggregate demand curve is not great enough to generate full employment.

XIX. SUMMARY

1. Eliminating the assumption that there is only one firm in the economy does not alter the NNP statement, but it does make it necessary to distinguish between a firm's output and it's true contribution to production. Since most firms buy raw materials from other firms, we would be counting the same goods twice if we added the output of all firms together to find GNP.

2. In order to eliminate this possibility of multiple counting, it was necessary to consider the value-added statement. This statement is found when purchases of raw materials are subtracted from both sides of the production statement. The number shown on the bottom of a firm's value-added statement is its true contribution to GNP.

If the value-added statements of all firms are combined, the GBP statement for the economy is obtained.

3. Gross private domestic investment (GPDI) is defined as the sum of all additions to buildings and equipment and changes in inventories. GBP is equal to consumption plus GPDI. It is also equal to the sum of all wages and salaries, rents, interest, depreciation, and profits.

4. Net private domestic investment (NPDI) is GPDI minus depreciation. It indicates the net change in the capital stock during a period of time.

5. If depreciation is subtracted from both sides of the GBP

statement and if it assumed that no production occurs within households, the NNP statement is found. NNP is equal to NPDI plus consumption. It is also equal to the sum of all wages and salaries, rents, interest, and profits. The latter sum is the national income. The NNP and the national income are identical.

6. Net private saving (NPS) is defined as national income minus consumption. If consumption is subtracted from both sides of the NNP statement, we see that NPDI is equal to NPS. This is an accounting identity; it is necessarily true.

7. Although saving is necessarily equal to investment, it must not be assumed that total demand necessarily equals NNP. If consumers do not spend their saving on capital goods or if they do not lend their saving to others who spend it on capital goods, aggregate demand will be less than NNP. If this occurs, NPDI will still be equal to NPS, but the investment will be undesired, and the economy will become depressed.

8. With wages and prices constant, aggregate supply of output is determined entirely by aggregate demand. If aggregate demand were to become greater than the output at full employment, however, this would no longer be true. Output would then be equal to the full-employment output, no matter how great demand is.

9. Demand for output consists of consumption demand plus investment demand. Consumption demand is a function of NNP. There are three laws of consumption.

(a) The marginal propensity to consume is a positive fraction.

(b) The average propensity to consume decreases as income increases.

(c) The average propensity to consume is greater than one at low levels of income.

10. Since saving is defined as the difference between income and consumption, the relationship of saving to income can be found from the relationship of consumption to income. The marginal propensity to save is equal to one minus the marginal propensity to consume. Corresponding to the three laws of consumption, there are, therefore, three laws of saving.

11. For output to be in equilibrium, the aggregate demand for output must equal NNP. When this is true saving equals investment demand.

12. An increase in investment demand or an increase in autonomous consumption leads to a multiple increase in NNP. To find the change in NNP you must multiply the change in ID or AC by the reciprocal of the marginal propensity to save or, which is the same thing, the reciprocal of one minus the marginal propensity to consume.

13. The classical economists believed that aggregate demand for output was always equal to NNP and that saving always equaled investment demand. Keynesian theory rejects this idea; it holds that this will only be true in equilibrium, and equilibrium may be at less than full employment. If enough output were produced to give everyone a job, aggregate demand might be less than NNP. Output would then decline until equilibrium was reached at less than full employment.

3

The Determinants of Investment Demand

According to the elementary version of the Keynesian theory of income determination, aggregate demand determines equilibrium NNP. Ignoring the existence of government and foreign trade, aggregate demand is separable into two components: consumption demand and investment demand. Consumption demand depends on the NNP. Given a relationship between consumption demand and the NNP, investment demand determines the NNP and employment. When investment demand is low, the NNP is low; when investment demand is high, the NNP is high.

But what determines investment demand—what makes it change? Thus far, investment demand has been treated as autonomous, although subject to variation. We have not discussed the factors that make it high or low—that make it change. Now we turn to these problems.

I. EXPECTATIONS AND INVESTMENT DEMAND

Investment is a gamble. Investors give up funds today to hold buildings, equipment, and inventories, hoping that tomorrow they well receive more than the cost of their investments. Consider, for example, investing in an apartment house. An investor in such a building anticipates receiving rental income in the future. The expected incomes, when compared to the cost of the building, decide the profitability of the investment. It is seldom possible to know what all of the future rents will be; one can only guess. Thus, expectations of future rents are important in determining the amount of desired investment in housing.

Expectations are also important in influencing inventory investment demand. When a retailer orders goods, he does not, as a rule, have a specific buyer for them; he buys in anticipation of a sale, not to fill an order. But there is no way to know, for sure, whether the goods can be sold at a profitable price. Therefore, whether the investment will be judged profitable depends on expectations of future demand conditions and future prices.

Finally, consider a manufacturer's decision to buy new machinery. He will know the cost of the machinery, but not the future profits that it will earn for him. The profitability of the machinery will depend, in part, on future demand and prices for his products, which are now imperfectly known. Investment demand for machinery, similarly, depends on expectations about future economic conditions.

To state that investment demand depends on expectations is not a satisfactory explanation of what determines investment demand. On what do expectations depend? Unfortunately, a complete answer is not possible. We do know, nonetheless, that the current state of the economy and the direction of movement in the economy play a significant role in the formation of expectations. If the national income is high, the profits earned on the existing capital stock will tend to be high. The favorable return to existing capital will lead many people to expect a continuing favorable return and will stimulate their desire to add more capital. If the NNP is low, current returns on capital will be low; pessimism about future returns will be likelier; and investment demand will be less.

Introduction of a relationship between investment demand and the NNP complicates the analysis in the previous chapter only slightly. Consider, for example, the following investment-demand function:

$$ID = AID + mpiNNP, \tag{3.1}$$

where *AID* is autonomous investment demand and *mpi* is *the marginal propensity to invest.* Since we are assuming that an increase in the *NNP* raises profits and, therefore, investment demand, *mpi* is positive.

If consumption demand (*CD*) is equal to autonomous consumption demand (*ACD*) plus the marginal propensity to consume (*mpc*) times the *NNP*, then aggregate demand (*AD*), the sum of *ID* and *CD*, can be stated as follows:

$$AD = AID + ACD + (mpi + mpc)\,NNP. \qquad (3.2)$$

Since *AD* will equal the *NNP* in equilibrium, equilibrium is found by substituting *NNP* for *AD* in Eq. 3.2 and solving for *NNP*.

$$NNP = \frac{1}{1 - (mpc + mpi)}\,(AID + ACD). \qquad (3.3)$$

The change in the *NNP* that will result from a dollar change in autonomous consumption demand or investment demand is no longer 1 over 1 minus the marginal propensity to consume. The multiplier is now 1 over 1 minus the sum of the marginal propensities to consume and invest. If we remember that the marginal propensity to save is 1 minus the marginal propensity to consume, we can write the multiplier as the reciprocal of the difference between the marginal propensity to save and the marginal propensity to invest.

If the marginal propensity to consume were 0.8 and the marginal propensity to invest 0.1, then the multiplier would be 10. An increase in either autonomous investment demand or autonomous consumption demand by $1 billion would increase equilibrium *NNP* by $10 billion.

QUESTIONS

1. What have expectations to do with a potential investor's decision to build a new shopping plaza? Would the profitability of existing shopping plazas influence his expectations? Would the profitability of existing shopping plazas depend in part on the NNP?
2. Assume that the marginal propensity to consume is 0.5 and that the marginal propensity to invest is 0.2.
   (a) Fill in the Table 3-1 and find equilibrium NNP.
   (b) Fill in Eq. 3.3 and find equilibrium NNP algebraically.

Table 3-1.

If NNP Is:	Consumption Demand Would Be:	Investment Demand Would Be:	Total Demand Would Be:	Saving Would Be:	NNP Would:
0	20	4	24	—20	Increase
20					
40	40	12	52	0	Increase
60					
80					
100					
120					

II. THE ACCELERATION PRINCIPLE

In addition to a high rate of NNP, *changes* in the NNP also influence investment demand. Even if income is low, firms may adjust their capital to the low level, so that if the NNP increases a deficiency of capital would be felt. In this case an increase in the NNP would induce new investment demand. Similarly, if output is high, it is possible that firms will adjust their capital stock (buildings, equipment, and inventories) to the high rate of output. Any decline in demand that may be expected to persist, even though demand is still great, would leave them with excess capital; and investment demand, if positive at all, would be small.

Consider, for example, a retail store that sells only men's shirts. On the average, the most profitable quantity of shirts to have on hand might be equal to one half of annual sales. If the firm expects sales of $20,000, it would want $10,000 in inventories. With $10,000 in its inventories, and sales of $20,000 a year, it would have no reason to invest in more inventories. As sales occur, it would buy shirts to maintain its inventories at the $10,000 level, but that would be all.

Now consider what would happen if sales increased to $21,000 a year. The firm would not only order shirts to replace those that have been sold, it would also order additional shirts to add to its inventories. If the sales were expected to remain at $21,000, it would want an inventory of $10,500 instead of $10,000. To increase its inventories it would have to invest. Thus, in this instance, the increase in sales by $1000 would result in investment demand of $500. It should be noted that if inventories were increased to this level and if sales were to remain at $21,000, there would be no further investment.

Not only would inventories depend on expected sales; so would the size of the store and the quantity of equipment to display the merchandise. If sales increased from $20,000 to $21,000 a year, the firm might desire a larger building and more equipment. However, once it adjusted the size of the store and the quantity of equipment to the new level of sales, investment in buildings and equipment would be zero.

The acceleration principle has been generalized to the whole economy. Instead of one firm's capital being related to its sales, the nation's capital stock is related to the NNP. Once the capital stock becomes appropriate for a given NNP, there would be no desire for further capital; investment demand would be zero. Only if NNP grew would there be investment demand. If the capital stock in equilibrium were four times the annual NNP and if this relationship held initially, a decrease in the NNP by $1 billion would imply $4 billion worth of excess capital. Investment demand would, therefore, be negative; firms would not replace some of their capital as it depreciated. If, however, the NNP were to remain unchanged rather than decrease, there would be no need for further capital; investment demand would be zero. According to the acceleration principle, only if the NNP were to grow would investment demand exist at all.

If the acceleration principle were all that were needed to explain investment demand, the NNP would be extremely unstable. Imagine, for example, that the NNP is approximately at the full-employment level for two years. If it does not rise during these two years, investment demand would be zero. But if investment demand were zero, the NNP would clearly decrease. If the NNP decreases, investment demand becomes negative, and the NNP falls still further. The failure of output to grow makes it decline precipitously. Only if the NNP is growing, and growing at the proper rate, would continuous full employment remain possible. According to this principle the economy cannot remain in equilibrium with a constant NNP; the NNP must grow, or the economy will collapse.

Although the acceleration principle contains an important element of truth, there is more to the investment process than the principle implies. Even if the NNP were to remain unchanged, there could still be incentives for investing. This is true for several reasons. First, the current rate of change in the economy is not a perfect index of future changes. Even if the NNP has not grown since last year, some investors could still expect increases in the future and would want to invest. Furthermore, if existing firms are earning good profits, there is an incentive for new firms to become established, even though the existing firms are able to satisfy all that is demanded. There is further incentive for existing firms to invest in new activities, even though the firms already engaged in those activities can supply all that is demanded.

It is also true that there is seldom an absolutely invariable relationship between capital and sales. If capital became less expensive relative to other costs, investment could occur as firms attempted to increase the amount of capital on hand to produce an unchanged output.

Finally, the acceleration principle abstracts from the introduction of new methods for producing old products and the introduction of new products. Even though firms may have sufficient capital to produce all that they expect to be able to sell, they may find it profitable to buy new capital to replace the old before it wears out. If the firms presently in an industry fail to do so, new firms may enter their industry, using the improved methods and, through competition, force the old firms out of business.

QUESTIONS

1. Imagine a manufacturing firm that uses $3 worth of machinery to produce each dollar's worth of yearly sales. If it must replace 10% of its machinery every year, how much replacement demand for machinery will it have each year if it were in equilibrium with sales of $1 million? If sales remain in equilibrium at $1 million, would there be a desire to add to the capital stock? What would happen if sales fell by $100,000? If they rose by $100,000?

2. Which one of the following statements is not a statement of the acceleration principle?
    (a) If NNP increases, investment demand will increase.
    (b) If NNP increases, investment demand will be positive.
    (c) If NNP increases, the desired capital stock will increase.
3. Give at least three reasons why a firm might want to invest, even though its sales this year were no higher than they were last year.

III. THE COST AND AVAILABILITY OF CREDIT

Another significant determinant of investment demand is the cost and availability of credit. A businessman who borrows to invest must consider the cost of borrowing when determining an investment's profitability. If borrowed money costs 5% a year, he would only undertake those investment projects that he anticipates will yield a rate of return higher than 5%. If the expected rate of return from investing were 4%, the investment would not be profitable; whereas if the expected return were 8%, it would be profitable.

Even businessmen who have enough money to invest without borrowing are affected by the rate of interest. Potential investors with available funds must compare the return that they could earn from lending with that to be earned from investing. Imagine, for example, someone who faces the alternatives of converting his funds into capital or lending to someone else. If he is to make the investment rather than the loan, he must believe that he will receive a rate of return greater than the rate of interest. If he expects a 5% rate of return from investing but could earn a 6% return by lending (the rate of interest is 6%), he lends rather than invests. However, if the rate of interest were 4%, then the investment that yielded 5% would be the better choice.

The higher the rate of interest, the smaller will be the number of investment projects that yield a rate of return greater than the rate of interest. The lower the rate of interest, the greater will be the number of investment projects that will yield a rate of return greater than the rate of interest. As the rate of interest falls, investment projects that were unprofitable at higher interest rates and would not have been undertaken become profitable, and are undertaken.

But, in addition to the rate of interest as an important determinant of investment demand, the availability of credit at existing interest rates is also important. Often people are not able to borrow as much as they want at existing interest rates because lenders ration the quantity of credit available. Credit rationing by lenders makes good sense. The more that a person or business firm is in debt, given net worth (assets minus liabilities), the greater is the chance that repayment will not be made. If, for example, someone has no wealth of his own (his assets equal his liabilities) but is able to borrow from others to acquire assets, those who lend to him have little protection against default. If his assets decline in value, he would then be unable to meet his obligations. If, on the other hand, someone is worth millions of dollars and has borrowed only a few hundred, the probability that he would be unable to pay would be infinitesimal. Consequently, someone may be able to borrow only $10,000 at a reasonable rate of interest, when he would like to have $20,000, simply because lenders do not believe that a further loan of $10,000 at the existing rate would be a good risk.

Although some borrowers may be unable to obtain as much credit as they would like at existing interest rates, they may be able to acquire more at some times than at others. If the interest rates of government securities fell, for example, a lender might be willing to make a larger loan to a borrower at 6% interest than he would have before. Since the alternative uses for the lender's funds have worsened, he is willing to take a little more risk at 6% than he would have previously. Similarly when interest rates are rising, credit rationing may become more stringent; the amount one could borrow at an unchanged rate of interest would become smaller as lenders are offered higher returns on funds placed elsewhere.

Thus, at any given time there are potential borrowers who believe that they could invest profitably if they only had the money. Although they believe they could make 7% by investment and the rate of interest is only 5%, they cannot carry through with this investment, because they cannot borrow all they want at 5%. If circumstances changed, however, then potential investors might be able to secure the money that they have desired all along, and investment demand would rise.

QUESTIONS

1. At what interest rates would you be willing to borrow to make an investment that will pay 7%?
2. If you did not have to borrow in order to invest, why would the rate of interest still be important to you in deciding the amount of your investments?
3. If there were $20 billion worth of investment projects that would be profitable at a rate of interest of 8% and if there were $5 billion worth that would be profitable at 7%, but not 8%, what would be the total value of profitable investment projects at 7%?
4. Why might you prefer to hold government bonds that pay 4% rather than lend to someone at 6%?
5. Imagine that you hold government securities and also make loans to businesses and individuals. Why might you be willing to lend more to individuals and businesses at 6% when interest rates on government securities were 3% than when they were 4%?

IV. SAVING AS A DETERMINANT OF INVESTMENT DEMAND

In Chapter 1 we discussed the classical view that investment demand is necessarily equal to saving. We argued that, given the way people behave and given our institutions, there are reasons why saving does not induce an equal amount of investment demand. Although saving and investment demand are not necessarily equal, it would be erroneous to argue that only changes in NNP equate them, that saving in no way induces investment demand, since there are usually individuals and businesses that would invest more if they had the funds to do so. Their desire to invest is thwarted by an inability to finance the investments.

Imagine someone, currently saving, who would invest more if he had the money. What will he do with his savings? Clearly he will use them for investment purposes. In this case, the act of saving leads to an increase in investment demand.

Of course, some saving is done by people who never invest or who believe that further investment is undesirable. They will not invest their saving. They may, however, lend all or part of it to those who believe that investment is profitable. Thus, much of saving may lead to investment demand.

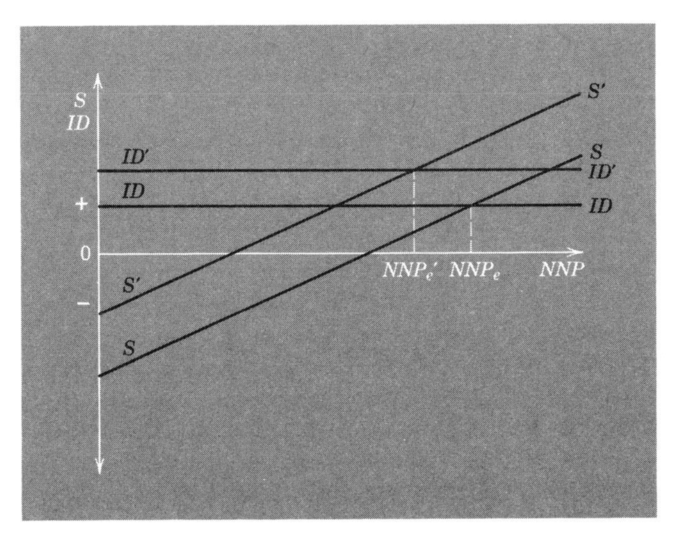

Figure 3-1

In the elementary version of the Keynesian theory of income determination presented in the previous chapter, investment demand was entirely autonomous. Such analysis can easily be modified to show the dependence of investment demand on saving. Consider Figure 3-1. *S-S* and *ID-ID* are the original saving-and-investment functions. Equilibrium *NNP* is NNP_e, the level of *NNP* at which saving is equal to investment demand. *S'-S'* and *ID'-ID'* are the saving-and-investment functions after an increase in the desire to save. Not only is the saving function shifted upwards so that more is saved at each income level, but the rate of desired investment is also greater at each income level. The change in saving at each income level is greater, however, than the change in investment demand; some of the saving does not lead to investment demand. The increase in the desire to save reduces the *NNP* to NNP_e'.

If investment demand does depend on saving, as we have maintained, then the analysis in the previous chapter gives the wrong *quantitative* result when considering the effects of a change in the desire to save; it implies that income would decrease more than it actually would. The elementary version of the Keynesian theory of income determination does give the right *qualitative* result, however; it says that NNP will decline, and it does. The classical analysis, in erroneously assuming that all that was saved would automatically lead to investment demand, implies that income would not change; this is not only the wrong quantitative result, it is the wrong qualitative one as well.

QUESTIONS

1. If you believe that the returns from investing are greater than the rate of interest, but you have been unable to invest because of an inability to borrow as much as you like, what would you do with your saving?
2. Why may those who wish to invest be able to borrow more when they save more?
3. If an increase in saving of $2 billion leads to an increase in investment demand of $1.5 billion, what happens to equilibrium NNP?

V. CONCLUSION

The theory of investment is one of the most complicated subjects in economics. Our discussion of it is by no means complete. We have, nonetheless, considered some of the most important factors influencing decisions to invest. One of these factors, the cost and availability of credit, will receive special attention in the following chapter. It will receive this attention not because we believe that this is the most important determinant of investment demand, but because the Federal Reserve authorities have some power to control it.

The NNP and change in the NNP may have more effect on investment demand than the cost and availability of credit. But it would do no good to suggest that full-employment NNP can be maintained by making the NNP high or by promoting a high rate of change of the NNP. One simply avoids the issue. How is the NNP to be controlled? If the Federal Reserve authorities can alter the cost and availability of credit, then they can manipulate this factor to achieve and maintain full-employment NNP.

VI. SUMMARY

1. There are numerous factors influencing decisions to invest. One of the most important ones is expectations. If the expected

returns on capital increase, investment demand is stimulated. If expected returns decrease, investment demand is discouraged. Although no complete explanation of expectations is available, the current return on capital is an important determinant of expected returns. When current returns are great, expected returns are likely to be great. Current returns depend importantly on the NNP. When the NNP is great, the capital stock is relatively scarce, and profits are high. But when the national income is low, capital is relatively abundant, and profits are low. Thus, a high NNP means a high-rate of investment demand; a low NNP means a low rate of investment demand.

2. In addition to the NNP itself, *changes* in the NNP may also be an important factor influencing investment demand. The relationship between changes in the NNP and investment demand is known as the "acceleration principle." If firms have adjusted their holdings of capital to the current rate of sales, whether sales are relatively great or relatively small, any change in sales will create either a shortage or excess of capital. Thus, if national income is increasing, investment demand will tend to be positive. If national income is not changing, then investment demand would tend to be zero. With investment demand zero, the NNP would fall to a low level. According to the acceleration principle, the NNP must grow or it will collapse.

3. In addition to income and changes in income influencing the rate of investment demand, the cost and availablity of credit affect it. The lower the cost of credit (interest rates), the more profitable investment projects there will be. The easier credit is to obtain at given interest rates, the more investment projects there will be that will be undertaken. Aggregate demand can, therefore, be stimulated by lowering the cost of credit and increasing its availability.

4. Saving is also a determinant of investment demand, although this is overlooked in the elementary version of the Keynesian theory of income determination that was presented in Chapter 2. If saving increases, those who believe that investment is profitable will use their saving to buy capital goods. They may also be able to borrow from those who do not believe that investment is the best use of savings, because their own saving has increased their wealth and made them a better risk. Whereas the elementary version of the Keynesian theory would give the wrong

quantitative answer to the question of what happens if the desire to save increases, it does give the correct qualitative conclusion. Since investment demand would not ordinarily rise by as much as saving, aggregate demand would decline and the NNP would fall. The important conclusions in the book are the qualitative ones. We are most concerned with knowing whether Y rises or falls when X is increased. An elementary theory that gives the right conclusions has much in its favor, even though more involved theories with more realistic assumptions are available.

4

Banking and Monetary Policy

The primary purpose of this chapter is to show how the authorities who control the Federal Reserve System can alter credit conditions and thereby control the NNP and level of employment. When the monetary authorities believe that aggregate demand is deficient, they can lower interest rates and increase the availability of credit; when they believe that aggregate demand is excessive, they can tighten credit and raise interest rates. How are they able to achieve these results?

In order to understand the powers that the Federal Reserve authorities have to control aggregate demand, it is first essential to understand the functioning of our commercial banking system. A *commercial* bank is any banking institution that has checking-account liabilities; these checking-account liabilities are called demand deposits. Demand deposits are the most important means of payment in our economy. Since by money we mean anything that is generally used as a means of payment, demand deposits are money. In fact, most of our money consists of demand deposits —balances held in checking accounts. In 1965 the total money supply in the United States was approximately $160 billion. Of this amount, $34 billion was coin and currency issued by either the Federal Reserve Banks or the Treasury, while the remaining $126 billion was demand deposit liabilities of commercial banks.

The nature of our commercial banking system can be more easily grasped by those who understand *condition statements*, also called balance sheets. A person's, business's, or bank's net worth (wealth) is defined as the difference between assets and liabilities. An individual's (or a firm's) assets are what he owns and what is owed to him. His liabilities are what he owes to others. To find out what someone is worth, we must subtract what he owes from what he owns and what is owed to him. Since net worth is equal to assets minus liabilities, assets necessarily equal liabilities plus net worth. A condition statement or balance sheet is simply an accounting statement that lists assets on the left side (debit side) and liabilities and net worth on the right side (credit side). Since assets are equal to liabilities plus net worth, the two sides must add up to the same thing.

If a person had $50 in cash, $100 owed to him, and owned $400 worth of clothing, books, radios, etc., his assets would be $550. If his only debt was a $150 loan owed to a bank, his total liabilities would also be $150. Subtracting liabilities from assets gives net worth; it would be $400. His condition statement would appear as shown in Table 4-1.

Table 4-1. Condition Statement

Assets:		*Liabilities:*	
Cash	$ 50	Bank loan	$150
Notes receivable	100	*Net worth:*	400
Other assets	400		
	$550	Total liabilities and net worth	$550

QUESTIONS

1. Could the statement in Table 4-2 be a condition statement for a commercial bank? Explain.

Table 4-2. Condition Statement

Assets:		*Liabilities:*	
Cash	$ 10	Savings deposits	$320
Loans and securities	355	*Net worth:*	45
	$365	Total liabilities and net worth	$365

2. Construct a condition statement from the following information. Two of the items are only listed to confuse.

Inventories	$ 55	Net worth	$145
Cash	50	Buildings and equipment	150
Other liabilities	100	Purchases of raw materials	20
Sales	860	Other assets	40
Notes payable	45	Wages owed	80
Notes receivable	75		

I. THE BARE ELEMENTS OF COMMERCIAL BANKING

There are approximately 13,500 commercial banks in the United States, and if branches were counted as separate institution there would be many more. To simplify the problem, we shall consider a consolidated condition statement for all commercial banks, rather than 13,500 separate statements. In effect, we treat all banks as if they were but branches of one great monopoly bank.

A consolidated condition statement for all the commercial banks in our economy, omitting any specific numbers, could appear as given in Table 4-3.

Table 4-3. Consolidated Condition Statement for All Commercial Banks

Assets:	*Liabilities:*
Coin and currency	Demand deposits of the public (D)
Demand deposits at the Federal Reserve Banks	Indebtedness to the Federal Reserve Banks (IF)
Loans and securities (LS)	Other liabilities (OL)
Other assets (OA)	
	Net worth: (NW)

If all commercial banks were members of the Federal Reserve System (although only about one-half of the banks are, the ones that do not belong are small), they would be required to hold *reserves* (R). A bank can count as reserves (R) its holdings of coin and currency and its demand deposits at its Federal Reserve Bank. The consolidated condition statement could then be shown as in Table 4-4.

Table 4-4. Consolidated Condition Statement for All Commercial Banks

Assets:	*Liabilities:*
R	D
LS	IF
OA	OL
	Net worth: (NW)

The reserves that a bank must hold are its *required reserves* (RR). Required reserves (RR) are a fraction of demand deposit liabilities (D). If we let r stand for the reserve requirement, then the following equation defines required reserves.

$$RR = rD. \quad (4.1)$$

If the commercial banks, as a whole, had $100 billion in demand deposit liabilities and if the reserve requirement were 15%, they would be required to have at least $15 billion in either cash or demand deposits at the Federal Reserve Banks. If the banks held more than $15 billion in reserves, they would have *excess reserves* (ER). Excess reserves (ER) are the difference between reserves (R) and required reserves (RR). This definition can be expressed in equation form.

$$ER = R - RR. \quad (4.2)$$

Although banks sometimes have excess reserves, this is usually evidence of disequilibrium. The primary source of income for commercial banks is the interest earned from their holdings of loans and securities; banks earn no interest on their reserves. If they have excess reserves they can buy more securities or make more loans and, therefore, earn more interest.

Given some amount of excess reserves, there is a limit to how much banks can increase their earning assets. Although banks, as a group, generally do not lose reserves when they make loans or buy securities, these actions nonetheless eliminate excess reserves because they lead to the creation of new demand deposits. When the commercial banking system buys securities or makes new loans, the checking accounts of the sellers or borrowers, whatever the case may be, are increased. Demand deposits grow.

Imagine, for example, that a bank makes a new loan of $10. Its assets increase by that amount, since someone would now owe it that much more. Its liabilities to the borrower would increase by the amount of the loan, since it would credit the account of the borrower. The changes in the consolidate condition statement for all commercial banks would be as follows:

Consolidated Condition Statement for All Commercial Banks

Assets:		*Liabilities:*	
LS	+10	D	+10

Although reserves have not changed, demand deposit liabilities have changed. Since required reserves are a fraction of demand deposit liabilities, lending has increased required reserves. With actual reserves unchanged, excess reserves have been reduced.

Thus we can conclude that when banks have excess reserves they buy more securities or lend more. This action increases their demand deposit liabilities and, therefore, their required reserves. The commercial banking system will only be in equilibrium when excess reserves have disappeared. The following equation states this equilibrium condition for the commercial banking system.

$$ER = O \qquad (4.3)$$

If Eqs. 4.1 to 4.3 are solved simultaneously, we obtain an equilibrium relationship among the demand deposit liabilities of commercial banks, their reserves, and the reserve requirement. It is

$$\mathrm{D} = \frac{R}{r} \qquad (4.4)$$

The consolidated condition statement for all commercial banks (Table 4-4) can be treated as an equation: the sum of the assets equals the sum of the liabilities plus net worth. Solving this equation for loans and securities, we find that

$$LS = D + IF + OL + NW - OA - R. \qquad (4.5)$$

Since in the analysis that follows we are not going to be interested in changes in other assets, other liabilities, or net worth of the commercial banks, it will simplify our discussion if we assume these items away. Let us pretend, therefore, that Eq. 4.5 can be written as

$$LS = D + IF - R. \qquad (4.6)$$

If Eq. 4.4 is now substituted into Eq. 4.6, we find that

$$LS = \frac{(1 - r)}{r} R + IF. \tag{4.7}$$

The total quantity of loans made by commercial banks and securities bought by them depends in a specific way on their reserves, the reserve requirement, and their indebtedness to the Federal Reserve Banks. This relationship will be of great use to us in learning how the Federal Reserve Banks can alter interest rates and the availability of credit.

QUESTIONS

1. What, if anything, happens to reserves if commercial banks deposit cash at the Federal Reserve Banks?
2. What, if anything, happens to reserves, required reserves, and excess reserves if banks buy securities, paying the sellers by crediting their checking accounts?
3. Given two condition statements (Table 4-5), prepare a consolidated condition statement.

Table 4-5.

Bank A				Bank B			
Assets:		*Liabilities:*		*Assets:*		*Liabilities:*	
R	$10	D	$100	R	$ 8	D	$80
LS	95	*Net worth:*	5	LS	76	*Net worth:*	4

4. Assuming that the reserve requirement is 10% and that the commercial banking system is in equilibrium, fill in the two missing items in the condition statement in Table 4-6.

Table 4-6. Consolidated Condition Statement for All Commercial Banks

Assets:		*Liabilities:*	
R	$ 20	D	$—
LS	210	IF	5
OA	15	OL	10
		Net worth:	—

5. (a) Assuming that the reserve requirement is 20% and that the commercial banking system is in equilibrium, fill in the two missing items in the condition statement in Table 4-7.

Table 4-7. Consolidated Condition Statement for All Commercial Banks

Assets:		*Liabilities:*	
R	$100	D	$—
LS	—	IF	10
OA	20	OL	5
		Net worth:	35

(b) Could LS and D be less than you have indicated in your answer to part *a* without the commercial banks violating any law? If yes, why would you ordinarily not expect them to be?

II. THE THREE INSTRUMENTS OF CREDIT CONTROL

In the United States those who control the Federal Reserve System have the power to alter credit conditions. The system consists of a Board of Governors located in Washington, D.C., and twelve Federal Reserve Banks, some of which have branches. The main decisions affecting credit conditions are made by the Board of Governors and the Open-Market Committee. This committee has twelve voting members, the seven members of the Board of Governors, who are appointed by the President of the United States for terms of fourteen years, and five presidents of Federal Reserve Banks.

The Federal Reserve authorities have three main instruments for altering credit conditions: (1) open-market operations, (2) variable reserve requirement, and (3) variable discount rate. By far the most important instrument is open-market operations.

Open-market operations refers to purchases and sales of government securities by the Federal Reserve Banks. The policy leading to decisions to buy or sell is made by the Open-Market Committee and is carried out by the Federal Reserve Bank of New York.

III. THE DIRECT EFFECTS OF OPEN-MARKET OPERATIONS

In order to understand how open-market operations alter credit conditions, consider what would happen if the Federal Reserve Bank of New York bought some government securities. The increased demand for securities would raise their price. With the price of the securities *higher,* the interest rate that they yield to their holders would *decrease*. If, for example, a bond promises to pay the holder $1100 one year from today and if it sells for $1000 today, then a purchaser of this security could expect a 10% return; he gets $100 interest on $1000 for one year. But if the price of the security were $1050 instead of $1000, then only $50 would be earned on $1050; the rate of return would then be approximately 4¾% – $50/$1050.

It is generally true that an increase in the price of a security that promises to pay a fixed sum of money in the future implies a reduction in the interest rate to be earned by buying that security. Similarly, a reduction in price implies an increase in the rate of interest.

When the "Fed," as the Federal Reserve System is often called, buys one type of government security, it not only raises the price of that security, lowering the interest that it yields, but its action tends to raise the price of all other securities, lowering the interest rates that they yield, as well. Why is this true? The reduction in the interest rate on the bonds bought by the Federal Reserve Bank makes them relatively less attractive sources of income. With the prices and yields of other securities initially unchanged, these other securities become relatively more attractive. Consequently, there would be a tendency for their prices to rise and the interest rate that they yield to fall, as more and more people demanded them instead of the security whose price rose initially.

The reduction in interest yields on existing securities, following the open-market purchases of government securities, would lower interest rates to new borrowers and increase the availability of credit to them at unchanged interest rates. Lenders who, prior to the Federal Reserve action, could earn 5% by holding bonds, now earn less, let us say 4%. Competition in the security markets will see to it that new borrowers will have to pay no more to obtain funds than old securities yield. If, for example, securities already in the market now yield 4%, no one who wished to issue a new security, entailing the same degree of risk as the old, need pay more than 4%. Thus the Fed's action in buying government securities lowers the interest yields on all existing securities and lowers the interest rate charged to new borrowers.

In addition to a decline in interest rates, more credit might be available to borrowers at unchanged interest rates. When lenders can earn 5% on government securities, they may be willing to lend at 6% only one half of the amount of money someone would like to borrow. But if the yield on government securities falls to 4%, then one might discover that one could obtain at an unchanged rate of interest more than one half of the amount one would like to borrow.

To sum up: the direct impact of open-market purchases of securities by the Federal Reserve Banks is to lower yields on existing securities, lower interest rates to new borrowers, and make credit at unchanged interest rates more available. Since investment demand depends, in part, on interest rates and the availability of credit, when the monetary authorities wish to stimulate the economy they can do this by buying securities. The reverse is clearly also true. When the authorities believe that total demand is excessive, they can, through open-market sales of government securities, lower investment demand by raising interest rates and reducing the availability of credit.

QUESTIONS

1. (a) What rate of return can be earned on a government security that promises to pay $1000 one year from today if it can be bought for $960?

   (b) What if it costs $970?
2. Assume that on January 1, 1960, the government sold for $1000 a bond promising to pay $40 on January 1, 1961, and then $1040 on January 1, 1962, when the security was to be retired.

   (a) What rate of interest did the government pay in order to borrow for two years?

   (b) If on January 1, 1961, just after the $40 interest was paid, the security sold for $1010, how much would the government have had to pay then to borrow for one year?
3. Why are not all interest rates the same?
4. Why do open-market purchases of one type of security affect the prices of all types of securities?
5. Why may a reduction in interest rates on government securities make it possible to borrow more at unchanged interest rates?

IV. THE REPERCUSSIONS OF OPEN-MARKET OPERATIONS ON COMMERCIAL BANKS

Not only do open-market operations tend directly to alter the cost and availability of credit, but their effects are also multiplied by the commercial banking system. When the Federal Reserve buys government securities, it makes it possible for the commercial banks also to buy more; the amount the commercial banks can buy is a multiple of the amount bought by the Fed.

Assume that the Federal Reserve Bank of New York buys a billion dollars worth of government securities with checks drawn against itself; these are called cashier checks. The sellers of the securities would deposit the checks in their commercial banks. The commercial banks would, in turn, deposit the checks at the Federal Reserve Banks. A consolidated condition statement for all commercial banks would show the changes indicated below:

Consolidated Condition Statement for All Commercial Banks

Assets:		*Liabilities:*	
Reserves (R)	+$1 billion	Demand deposits of the public (D)	+$1 billion

From the point of view of the commercial banks, the important result of the open-market purchase by the Federal Reserve Banks is that their reserves have increased as much as their demand deposit liabilities. If the reserve requirements is a fraction, and it is, and if the banks were fully loaned up to begin with, having neither excess nor deficient reserves, the banks would now have excess reserves. If the reserve requirement were 20%, for example, they would need $200 million more in reserves to cover their new demand deposit liabilities of $1 billion. But the banks have $1 billion in new reserves. They have, therefore, $800 million in excess reserves and can buy more securities or make more loans.

To what extent can they increase their earning assets? If they increased their loans and holdings of securities by $800 million, paying with demand deposits, they would still have excess reserves. To see that this is true, consider again what the changes would be in the consolidated condition statement for all commercial banks if the commercial banks increased their earning assets this amount.

Consolidated Condition Statement for All Commercial Banks

Assets:		*Liabilities:*	
R	+$ 1 billion	D	+$ 1 billion
LS	+$800 million		+$800 million

The total increase in demand deposits has been \$1.8 billion, \$1 billion because of the original purchase of securities by the Federal Reserve Banks and \$800 million because the commercial banks bought securities or made new loans. With demand deposit liabilities up by \$1.8 billion, the commercial banks would have to have 20% of that (\$360 million) in reserves. But their reserves are up by \$1 billion, so they still would have excess reserves; they would now have \$720 million. They could, therefore, expand their loans and security purchases further. Just how much could they increase their earning assets?

Equation 4.7 will answer this question for us. With r equal to 0.2, $(1-r)/r$ would be 4. Since indebtedness to the Federal Reserve Banks (IF) is unchanged and R has increased by \$1 billion, commercial banks as a whole could expand their loans and increase their holdings of securities by \$4 billion.

Clearly the major impact of open-market operations by the Federal Reserve Banks comes from the repercussions on the activity of the commercial banks. If the Fed buys \$1 billion worth of securities, this alone lowers interest rates and increases the availability of credit. But the commercial banks are than able to buy billions of dollars worth of securities or make billions of dollars of new loans and reinforces the action of the Federal Reserve Banks by a multiple.

QUESTIONS

1. Assume that the Federal Reserve Banks sell \$500 worth of securities to the public, that the public pays with checks drawn against commercial banks, and that the Federal Reserve Banks collect by reducing the accounts of the commercial banks.

   (a) Show how this transaction would alter the consolidated condition statement for all commercial banks.

   (b) Assuming that the reserve requirement is 10% and that the banks do not keep excess reserves, indicate the full alteration the above transaction would cause in the condition statement.

2. You will have shown, in answering Question 1*a*, a reduction in the demand deposits of the public. These deposits are the most important component of our money supply. If someone asked you where the money went, what would you say?

V. VARIABLE RESERVE REQUIREMENT

Although the Federal Reserve authorities rely primarily on open-market operations to control credit conditions and through them aggregate demand, they have other instruments that they can and do use from time to time. The Board of Governors can alter the reserve requirement.

If commercial banks tend not to keep excess reserves, any action by Federal Reserve authorities to create excess or deficient reserves will alter the amount of loans made and securities held by commercial banks. When reserve requirements are lowered, banks possessing the necessary amount of reserves would then have excess reserves. The excess reserves would permit them to buy more securities or make more loans. The cost and availability of credit would be altered and the economy stimulated.

If lowering the reserve requirement reduces the cost of credit and increases its availability, increasing the reserve requirement has the opposite effects. When the Board of Governors wishes to contract spending by tightening credit, it can do so by raising the reserve requirement. An increase in the requirement means that banks, given unchanged demand deposit liabilities, must have more cash or deposits at the Federal Reserve Banks. In an attempt to obtain additional reserves, they would sell securities, call loans, and make fewer loans as loans are paid off. People would pay with demand deposits, and these deposits would disappear. Credit would become tighter.

The influence of the reserve requirement on the quantity of loans made and securities held by the commercial banks can be seen from a further examination of Eq. 4.7. If we ignore the indebtedness of the commercial banks to the Federal Reserve Banks, IF becomes zero and Eq. 4.7 states that the earning assets of the commercial banks equal $(1-r)/r$ times the reserves of the banks. If the reserve requirement is lowered, $(1-r)/r$ becomes greater. With actual reserves unchanged, commercial bank loans and security holdings would incerase; credit would become cheaper and easier to obtain. Suppose the reserve requirement was 20%; when the reserves were $25 billion, then loans and securities would be $100 billion. If the reserve requirement was reduced to 19%, then the earning assets of the commercial banks would grow by over $6 billion. The lower the reserve requirement, the more credit the banks can extend; the greater the reserve requirement, the less.

QUESTIONS

1. If the reserve requirement increases, each bank tries to get more reserves by selling securities, calling loans, or failing to make new loans as old loans come due. Explain why a bank that sells securities might receive more reserves. Explain, also, why this would not mean an increase in reserves for all banks. If you have difficulty answering this question, it might help to imagine that there are only two banks and to use condition statements for them to show how each bank is affected by the transaction.
2. Using Eq. 4.7, show how great LS would be if R were $20 billion, IF $2 billion, and r 10%. How is the answer altered if r is 20%?

VI. VARIABLE DISCOUNT RATE

The Federal Reserve has a further instrument of control. It is the variable discount rate. To understand its force, consider first what happens to credit conditions if the commercial banks borrow from the Federal Reserve Banks.

If a commercial bank borrows $100,000 from a Federal Reserve Bank it would receive either $100,000 in cash or a $100,000 credit to its demand-deposit account at its Federal Reserve Bank. In either case, its reserves would increase by the amount of the loan. Its liabilities would be up by the same amount, and would show on its condition statement as an increase in its indebtedness to its Federal Reserve Bank. The consolidated condition statement for all commercial banks would be altered as follows:

Consolidated Condition Statement for All Commercial Banks

Assets:		*Liabilities:*	
R	**+$100,000**	**IF**	**+$100,000**

The entire increase in reserves represents an increase in excess reserves, since, with demand-deposit liabilities unchanged, required reserves would remain unchanged. The existence of excess reserves would permit commercial banks to expand their loans and holdings of securities by a multiple of their excess reserves. Again, Eq. 4.7 can be used to determine the size of the multiple.

If the reserve requirement were 20%, then $(1-r)/r$ would be 4. LS would equal four times reserves plus the banks' indebtedness to the Fed. Since R and IF have each increased by $100,000, the increase in earning assets would be $500,000, four times the increase in reserves plus the increase in indebtedness to the Fed.

In general, each dollar borrowed by a commercial bank permits an expansion of lending in the commercial banking system equal to the reciprocal of the reserve requirement. Equation 4.7 tells us that the change in LS equals $(1-r)/r$ times the change in R plus the change in IF. Since the change in R, when the banks borrow from the Fed, equals the change in IF, IF can be substituted for R in Eq. 4.7. As a consequence, the change in LS will equal $(1 - r)/r$ times the change in IF plus the change in IF. This reduces to $1/r$ times the change in IF.*

If the Federal Reserve Banks were willing to lend freely to the commercial banks at a zero rate of interest, the Federal Reserve authorities would have no control over credit conditions and the money supply. So long as the yield on securities was above zero, commercial banks would continue to borrow from the Federal Reserve Banks. No loan that was expected to return a positive rate of interest would be refused, because the funds necessary to make it could be obtained freely from the Federal Reserve Banks.

But the Federal Reserve Banks are not willing to lend unlimited amounts without cost. They charge a rate of interest on all loans.

---

* $$\Delta LS = \frac{(1-r)}{r}\Delta R + \Delta IF$$

$$\Delta IF = \Delta R$$

$$\Delta LS = \frac{(1-r)}{r}\Delta IF + \Delta IF$$

$$= \frac{(1-r)\ \Delta IF + r\Delta IF}{r}$$

$$= \frac{\Delta IF}{r}$$

This rate is called the *discount rate*. When the Federal Reserve authorities wish to discourage borrowing from the Federal Reserve Banks they can raise this rate. If they wished to encourage borrowing from the Fed, they can lower the rate. Since the discount rate will control, to some degree, the indebtedness of the commercial banks to the Federal Reserve Banks, and this indebtedness, in turn, controls, to some degree, the cost and availability of credit, varying the discount rate is an additional means at the monetary authorities' disposal to control aggregate demand.

QUESTIONS

1. Why, if there were but a single commercial bank, might the discount rate have to be above the yield on government securities in order to control credit? (*Hint.* How much could a monopoly commercial bank lend if it borrowed from the Federal Reserve Banks?)
2. Prove that an increase in the indebtedness of the commercial banks to the Federal Reserve Banks leads to a multiple increase in the earning assets of the commercial banks equal to the reciprocal of the reserve requirement.
3. Assume that, at the existing discount rate, commercial banks do not wish to increase their indebtedness to the Fed. Why might the Fed, nonetheless, have to increase the discount rate in order to limit commercial bank borrowing if it raised the reserve requirement?

VII. LIMITATIONS OF FEDERAL RESERVE POWER

Although the Federal Reserve authorities have sufficient power to keep aggregate demand from becoming excessive, their power to prevent deficient demand may be insufficient. This can be made clear by reconsidering the instruments that the Federal Reserve authorities have to control the cost and availability of credit: open-market operations, a variable reserve requirement, and a variable discount rate.

We have shown that a purchase of government securities raises their prices, lowering their yields, and then affects the prices and yields of all other securities. But if yields on securities become so low that virtually everyone is indifferent to the choice between holding interest-earning assets or money, even massive purchases of government securities by the Federal Reserve Banks may have an insignificant effect on interest rates. Under these circumstances the excess reserves created for the commercial banks through open-market purchases may not lead them to buy more securities or make more loans. They might simply keep these reserves.

Reductions in the reserve requirement and the discount rate create excess reserves for the commercial banks in the first case, and make it less expensive for the banks to obtain excess reserves in the second case. But if the yield on existing securities is so low that banks no longer have an incentive to buy them or make new loans, lowering the reserve requirement or reducing the discount rate would not reduce the cost or increase the availability of credit.

There were times during the 1930s when interest rates were extremely low, and banks held large amounts of excess reserves. For a while, treasury bills (the shortest-term government securities) earned their holders virtually no interest at all. And, in 1935, when the commercial banks that belonged to the Federal Reserve System held approximately $6 billion in reserves, one half of all reserves were excess.

What we must conclude is that the Federal Reserve authorities normally have the power to control the cost and availability of credit and, therefore, aggregate demand. In circumstances of extreme depression, however, interest rates may be so low that the powers of the Fed vanish. Maintenance of a sufficiently high level of aggregate demand, then, requires some other means of control. Varying government demand and taxes can fulfill this need. How the government can control economic activity by changing its expenditures and tax receipts is the subject of the next chapter.

QUESTIONS

1. Since it takes time and money to buy securities, why must the yield on securities be positive if anyone is to buy them?
2. If the yield on securities is positive, but only slightly above an absolute minimum, would it make sense any longer to claim that the Fed can lower interest rates?

VIII. SUMMARY

1. The Federal Reserve authorities can alter the cost and availability of credit. To appreciate the full impact of their actions, one must understand the nature of our fractional reserve commercial banking system. Assuming that commercial banks keep no excess reserves (ER), there is a formula relating the earning assets of the commercial banks (LS) to the reserve requirement (r), reserves (R), and commercial bank indebtedness to the Federal Reserve Banks (IF). It is: $LS = [(1 - r)/r]\, R + IF$.

2. The Federal Reserve authorities have three main instruments for controlling the cost and availability of credit. They are: (1) open-market operations, (2) variable reserve requirement, and (3) variable discount rate.

3. Open-market operations refer to the purchase and sale of government securities by the Federal Reserve Banks. When they buy government securities, the prices of the securities rise, and the interest rate that they yield falls. The interest yields of all securities are interrelated and, therefore, all interest rates tend to fall when the action of the Fed lowers any one of them. Thus, open-market purchases lower the cost and increase the availability of credit. Open-market operations have repercussions on the commercial banks; their major effects stem from the reaction of the commercial banks to the excess reserves that an open-market purchase creates. When the Fed buys government securities, the reserves of the commercial banks rise by the amount of the purchase. Since their indebtedness to the Fed is unaffected, their ability to buy securities and make loans is increased by a multiple of the purchase; the multiple is one minus the reserve requirement divided by the reserve requirement. Since the reserve requirement is a small fraction, less than one half, the earning assets of the commercial banks rise by more than the amount of the open-market purchase. The major effect of open-market operations results from actions of the commercial banks.

4. Changing the reserve requirement is an alternative means that the Federal Reserve authorities have to alter the cost and availability of credit. If the reserve requirement is reduced, previously required reserves become excess, and the banks can in-

crease their loans and buy more securities. Credit becomes cheaper and easier to obtain. When a reduction in aggregate demand is desired, the reserve requirement can be increased.

5. Finally, the Federal Reserve authorities can change the discount rate. This is the rate charged commercial banks when they borrow from the Federal Reserve Banks. For each dollar any one bank borrows from the Federal Reserve, the commercial banks, as a whole, can expand their loans and securities by the reciprocal of the reserve requirement. Since the reserve requirement is a fraction, the earning assets of the commercial banks, as a whole, rise by a multiple of their borrowings from the Federal Reserve. A rise in the discount rate discourages such borrowing; a decrease encourages it.

6. Although the power of the Federal Reserve to prevent excessive demand is sufficiently great, its power to maintain sufficient aggregate demand may be too limited. The Federal Reserve authorities control spending by controlling the cost and availability of credit. Whereas they may be able to make the cost of credit greater and reduce its availability, they may not always be able to do the reverse. There is a minimum below which interest rates cannot fall. If interest rates are already at that minimum or close to it, then the cost of credit cannot be significantly reduced. Furthermore, the creation of excess reserves for the commercial banks, by any of the instruments that the Federal Reserve authorities use, need not lead to an increase in either securities bought or loans made by commercial banks. The banks can keep excess reserves, and will do so if interest rates become very low.

7. If aggregate demand cannot always be controlled by the monetary authorities, then some other means of control is needed. Variation in government demand and taxes is an alternative means of control, as we shall show in the next chapter.

5

Fiscal Policy and the National Debt

The Keynesian theory of income determination, developed in Chapter 2, contained an unrealistic assumption. In that theory, aggregate demand had only two components: consumption demand and investment demand. There was no government to demand goods and services; there were no taxes to pay. But our government can and does buy goods and services, and also collects taxes. These actions by government affect the net national product. Let us now alter the elementary Keynesian theory to include government.

I. THE STATEMENT OF GROSS NATIONAL PRODUCT

Recall the statement of product created within the business sector, as derived in Chapter 2. It had two sides. On the left appeared sales to households and gross private domestic investment (GPDI) while, on the right, appeared wages and salaries, rent, and interest paid by the business sector, plus business profits. With government included, we must revise the statement. Sales can be made to the government, and businesses can have an additional cost: indirect business taxes (IBT).

Table 5-1 is a new statement of product created within the business sector. On the left, in addition to the two items that previously appeared, are sales to government. On the right, in addition to the items that previously appeared, are indirect business taxes (IBT). These taxes are taxes other than those on incomes; they include excise, sales, and real estate taxes. Social security taxes, corporate profits taxes, and personal income taxes are not included in IBT, since they are taxes on income. Although they do not appear explicitly in the statement, they are there, nonetheless. They are part of wages and salaries, rent, interest, and profits.

Table 5-1. Statement of Product Created within the Business Sector in the Absence of Foreign Trade

Sales to households	Indirect business taxes (IBT)
Sales to government	Wages and salaries
GPDI	Rent
	Interest
	Depreciation
	Profits
Gross product created in business sector	Gross product created in business sector

To find the GNP we must also determine the product created within the household and government sectors. If we value the product created within households by the amount of wages and salaries paid by them to domestic servants, the statement of product created within households appears as follows:

Statement of Product Created within Households

Expenditures on the services of domestics	Wages and salaries

The product created within the government sector is determined the same way as the product created within households. National income accountants compute it by adding together all wages and salaries paid by government. The product created by the President of the United States is equal to his salary. The product created by the U.S. Army is all of the salaries paid to those in and working for the Army. The product of the public school teachers of America is equal to the sum of all of their salaries.

The statement of product created within the government sector is then:

Statement of Product Created within the Government Sector

Government expenditures on personnel	Wages and salaries

To find the GNP we must sum the product created in the three sectors. We can do this by combining the three statements. The left side in such a combined statement will contain sales to households by the business sector and expenditures of households on the services of domestics. These may be combined and their sum called consumption expenditures (C). Sales to government by the business sector and expenditures of government on personnel also appear on the left side of the combined statements. Their sum is called government expenditures (G). The statements of the gross national product is thus given in Table 5-2.

Table 5-2. Statement of Gross National Product in Absence of Foreign Trade

Consumption expenditures (C)	IBT
Government expenditures (G)	Wages and salaries
GPDI	Rent
	Interest
	Depreciation
	Profits
Gross national product	Gross national product

By subtracting depreciation from both sides of the statement of gross national product, the statement of net national product (Table 5-3) emerges.

Table 5-3. Statement of Net National Product in Absence of Foreign Trade

Consumption expenditures (C)	IBT
Government expenditures (G)	Wages and salaries
GPDI—depreciation = NPDI	Rent
	Interest
	Profits
Net national product	Net national product

QUESTIONS

1. If the business sector sold $350 billion worth of goods to the household sector and if households spent $25 billion on the services of domestics, what was C?
2. If the business sector sold $20 billion worth of goods to the government sector and if the government sector spent $30 billion paying wages and salaries, what was G?

3. From the following information, compute the NNP two ways. C = 300; profits = 50; GPDI = 60; interest = 5; IBT = 10; depreciation = 20; G = 60; rent = 15; wages and salaries = 320.
4. Why does not the NNP statement show taxes other than IBT?

II. THE RELATIONSHIP BETWEEN SAVING AND INVESTMENT

There is another concept of income, called disposable income (DY), which we must introduce. Disposable income (DY) is the amount of income that households have available either to consume or save. It differs from the NNP and is, generally, less than it. Indirect business taxes, which are a part of the NNP, are not paid to households; they are paid to government. They are not, therefore, part of DY. In addition to IBT there are other taxes: social security taxes (SST), corporate profits taxes (CPT), and personal income taxes (PYT). All of these taxes must be subtracted from the NNP to find DY.

There is one item that must be added to NNP to compute DY; it is government transfer payments (GTP). These payments consist of interest on the national debt, veteran benefits, assistance to the poor, etc. They differ from other forms of income, since they are not generated in the process of production. If they were, they would be included in the NNP.

Finally, retained earnings of corporations (RE) must be subtracted from the NNP to arrive at DY. Although households, as shareholders of corporations, have earned this income, it is not available for consumption purposes, since businesses retain it.

The relationship between the *NNP* and *DY* can be summarized by the following equation:

$$DY = NNP - IBT - SST - CPT - PYT + GTP - RE \quad (5.1)$$

Household saving (HS) is defined as the difference between *DY* and *C*; it is the part of *DY* that is not consumed. It follows from this definition that *HS* plus *C* equals *DY*. If the sum of *HS* and *C* is substituted for *DY* in Eq. 5.1 and if the equation is then solved for *NNP*, we find that

$$NNP = C + HS + IBT + SST + CPT + PYT - GTP + RE. \quad (5.2)$$

The sum of *IBT*, *SST*, *CPT*, and *PYT* can be called simply taxes (T). If *GTP* are subtracted from taxes (T), we have a new concept; it is net taxes (NT), gross taxes minus transfers. Therefore, we can rewrite Eq. 5.2 as

$$NNP = C + HS + NT + RE. \tag{5.3}$$

RE is simply net business saving (net of depreciation). If it is added to *HS*, we have net private saving (*NPS*). Thus

$$NNP = C + NPS + NT. \tag{5.4}$$

Since we know from the statement of the net national product (Table 5-3) that the *NNP* is equal to C plus *NPDI* plus G, it follows from this and Eq. 5.4 that

$$NPDI + G = NPS + NT. \tag{5.5}$$

To increase our understanding of Eq. 5.5 and to convince ourselves that it is simply an accounting identity, consider a few transactions that might at first sight appear to affect one side of that equation more than another.

A. *Someone Buys a Tube of Toothpaste for 89¢*

The buyer's saving is down by 89¢, since he has increased his consumption by that amount. The saving of the retailer is probably up. If the toothpaste cost him 50¢ and if he valued his inventories at cost, the sale of the product for 89¢ earns him a profit. If 9¢ of the price goes to the government as an excise tax and if we ignore income taxes, his profit is 30¢; 89¢ minus the cost of the toothpaste to him (50¢) and minus the excise tax (9¢). Since the retailer has additional income of 30¢ that he has not consumed, his saving is up 30¢. Saving in the community is, therefore, down by 59¢; one person's is down by 89¢ but someone else's is up 30¢.

NPDI is also altered. Inventories valued at 50¢ have been reduced. Therefore, *NPDI* is down 50¢.

Finally, we must note that *NT* are up 9¢, the excise tax. The changes in each of the items in Eq. 5.5 is summarized below. We see that the sum of the changes on each side are equal.

$$\underset{NPDI}{(-50¢)} + \underset{G}{(0)} = \underset{NPS}{(-59¢)} + \underset{NT}{(+9¢)}$$

B. *A Government Agency Buys \$1 Million Worth of Pencils*

Government expenditures (G) would be up by \$1 million. If the pencils had cost the seller \$.7 million, his inventories would be down this much and, therefore, *NPDI* would be reduced by \$.7 million. What about *NPS* and *NT*?

The sale of the pencils has earned the seller a profit of \$.3 million. If we ignore all taxes, then *NPS* would be up \$0.3 million, since the seller has that much more income which he has not consumed. The changes could then be summarized as follows:

$$\underset{NPDI}{(-0.7)} + \underset{G}{(+1)} = \underset{NPS}{(+0.3)} + \underset{NT}{(0)}$$

If we assume that income taxes must be paid on the profits, the equality will still hold, since we will then transfer part of the *NPS* to *NT*. If, for example, 40% of additional profits are paid in taxes, then *NPS* would be up only 60% of \$0.3 million, while *NT* would be up 40% of \$0.3 million. The changes could then be summarized as follows:

$$\underset{NPDI}{(-0.7)} + \underset{G}{(+1)} = \underset{NPS}{(+0.18)} + \underset{NT}{(+0.12)}$$

QUESTIONS

1. (a) From the information below, compute DY, HS, and NPS. NNP = 400; RE = 10: SST = 15; GTP = 25; PYT = 30; CPT = 20; IBT = 5; C = 300.

   (b) What must the sum of G and NPDI be?

2. In each instance below indicate by exactly how much NPDI, G, NPS, and NT are changed.

   (a) You attend a movie, paying \$0.75, \$0.05 of which is an excise tax. Ignore income taxes.

   (b) You pay \$6 for a cotton shirt that cost the retailer \$4. The retailer pays 25% of his profits in income taxes.

   (c) A local government buys \$5 million worth of textbooks from a publisher. The textbooks, which were in the stocks of the publisher, cost \$3 million to print. The publisher pays the author 10% of the selling price. The author is in a 30% income tax bracket; the publisher is in a 50% bracket.

III. AGGREGATE DEMAND WITH GOVERNMENT DEMAND INCLUDED

Now that we have introduced government into national income accounting, we can turn to the theory. The existence of a government that spends and taxes does not alter the aggregate supply function. *NNP* will still be equal to aggregate demand (*AD*) in equilibrium. It is on the demand side that government makes a difference. Government demand (*GD*) must be included in *AD*.

$$AD = CD + ID + GD. \tag{5.6}$$

It will be an enormously useful simplification in the analysis that follows to assume that both *ID* and *GD* are constants. We shall examine the consequences of changes in them, but they will not be made functions of other variables. With *ID* and *GD* assumed constant, *CD* remains to be explained.

IV. CONSUMPTION DEMAND

In Chapter 2, *CD* was related to the *NNP*. Since we assumed there that there were no taxes to pay and no retained earnings, the *NNP* was necessarily equal to *DY*. In relating *CD* to the *NNP* we were relating it as well to *DY*. Once we introduce taxes, *NNP* and *DY* are no longer equal. Which, then, is *CD* to be related to, *DY* or *NNP*?

It is generally believed that *DY*, not *NNP*, is the most important determinant of *CD*. It is, after all, *DY* that is available to households to either consume or save. In the following analysis, therefore, *CD* will be assumed to depend on *DY*.

If we approximate the relationship between *CD* and *DY* with a linear function, as we did in Chapter 2, the consumption function can be written as

$$CD = AC + mpcDY, \tag{5.7}$$

where *AC* is autonomous consumption demand and *mpc* is the marginal propensity to consume out of disposable income.

If we ignore business saving (retained earnings) in order to

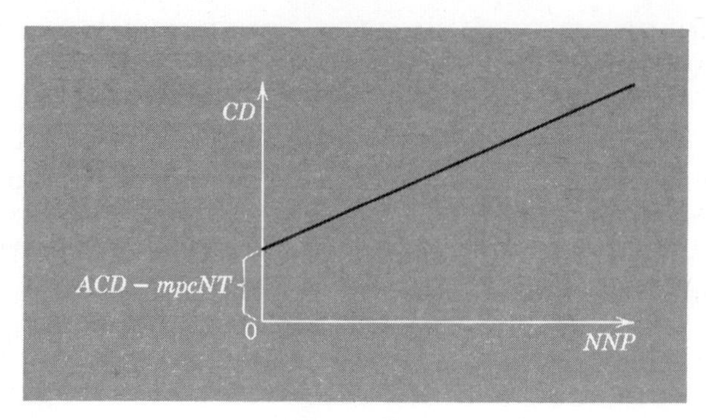

Figure 5-1

prevent the analysis from becoming too complicated, DY differs from the NNP by net taxes. We, therefore, have

$$DY = NNP - NT. \tag{5.8}$$

If Eq. 5.8 is solved simultaneously with Eq. 5.7 we obtain a relationship between CD and NNP; it is

$$CD = (AC - mpcNT) + mpcNNP. \tag{5.9}$$

Treating NT as autonomously determined, this function can be plotted on a diagram with CD on the vertical axis and NNP on the horizontal. It is shown in Figure 5-1. The vertical intercept of the function is $(AC - mpcNT)$, which is what CD would be if there were no NNP. The slope of the function is the marginal propensity to consume.

V. THE DIAGRAM OF AGGREGATE DEMAND AND AGGREGATE SUPPLY

We can now draw AD and AS functions, much as we did in Chapter 2. In Figure 5-2 AD is plotted on the vertical axis and AS on the horizontal. Three lines appear in the diagram. One is the AS function; it states that NNP will equal AD in equilibrium, so long as AD is equal to or less than full-employment NNP, NNP_f. Another line is the CD function; it is drawn exactly as it appeared in Figure 5-1. The third line is the AD function. It is drawn parallel to the CD function and is obtained by adding ID

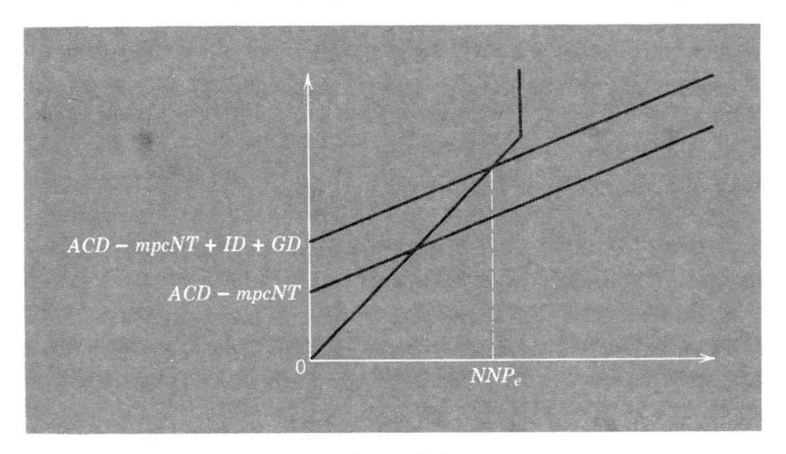

Figure 5-2

and *GD* to *CD*. Since *ID* and *GD* are both assumed to be constant, their sum is a constant. Thus, *AD* is greater than *CD* by this constant amount.

Equilibrium *NNP* is found at the point at which the *AD* and the *AS* function intersect; only at that point will the *NNP* equal *AD*. If *NNP* is greater than this, *AD* will be less than *NNP; NNP* and employment will decrease. If *NNP* is less than this, *AD* will be greater than *NNP; NNP* and employment will increase.

We can now consider what effect an increase in *GD* will have on equilibrium *NNP* and employment. If *GD* increases, the intercept of the *AD* function will move up, away from the origin, as shown in Figure 5-3. Equilibrium *NNP* rises by a multiple of the increase in *GD*. The effect of an increase in *GD* is exactly the same as that which follows an increase in either *ID* or autonomous *CD*. The intercept of the *AD* function will rise by exactly the amount of increase in *GD, ID,* or autonomous *CD*.

A *reduction* in taxes will also increase equilibrium *NNP*, but by less than an equivalent *increase in GD, ID,* or *ACD*. The intercept of the *AD* line depends on *NT*, but notice that *NT* is multiplied by the negative of the marginal propensity to consume. Since the marginal propensity to consume is a fraction, a reduction in *NT* will increase the intercept by less than the tax reduction. If *NT* fall by $10, the intercept of the *AD* function rises by the marginal propensity to consume times $10. If the

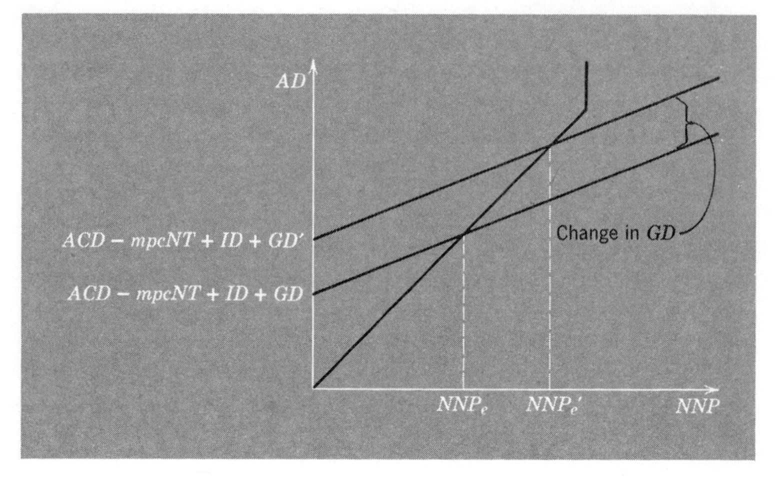

Figure 5-3

marginal propensity to consume is 0.8, then the intercept increases by $8 rather than $10.

If an economy is depressed, operating at less than full employment, equilibrium *NNP* and employment can be achieved by increasing *GD* or reducing taxes. If the monetary authorities do not wish to reduce the cost of credit and increase its availability, or if they are unable to do this, the government through decisions to tax and spend can pursue the goal of a job for everyone ready, willing, and able to work through the undertaking of public projects such as highways, buildings, and social programs, and the purchase of various goods and services from private sources.

QUESTIONS

1. Assuming that *ACD* is $15 billion, the marginal propensity to consume out of *DY* is 0.5, and *NT* are $10 billion, carefully draw in the consumption function on the graph on the next page.
2. Assuming that *ID* is $4 billion and *GD* is $11 billion, carefully draw in the *AD* and *AS* functions. What is equilibrium *NNP*?
3. Explain why, with reference to the diagram, a $1 billion reduction in *NT* will increase equilibrium *NNP* by less than a $1 increase in *GD*.

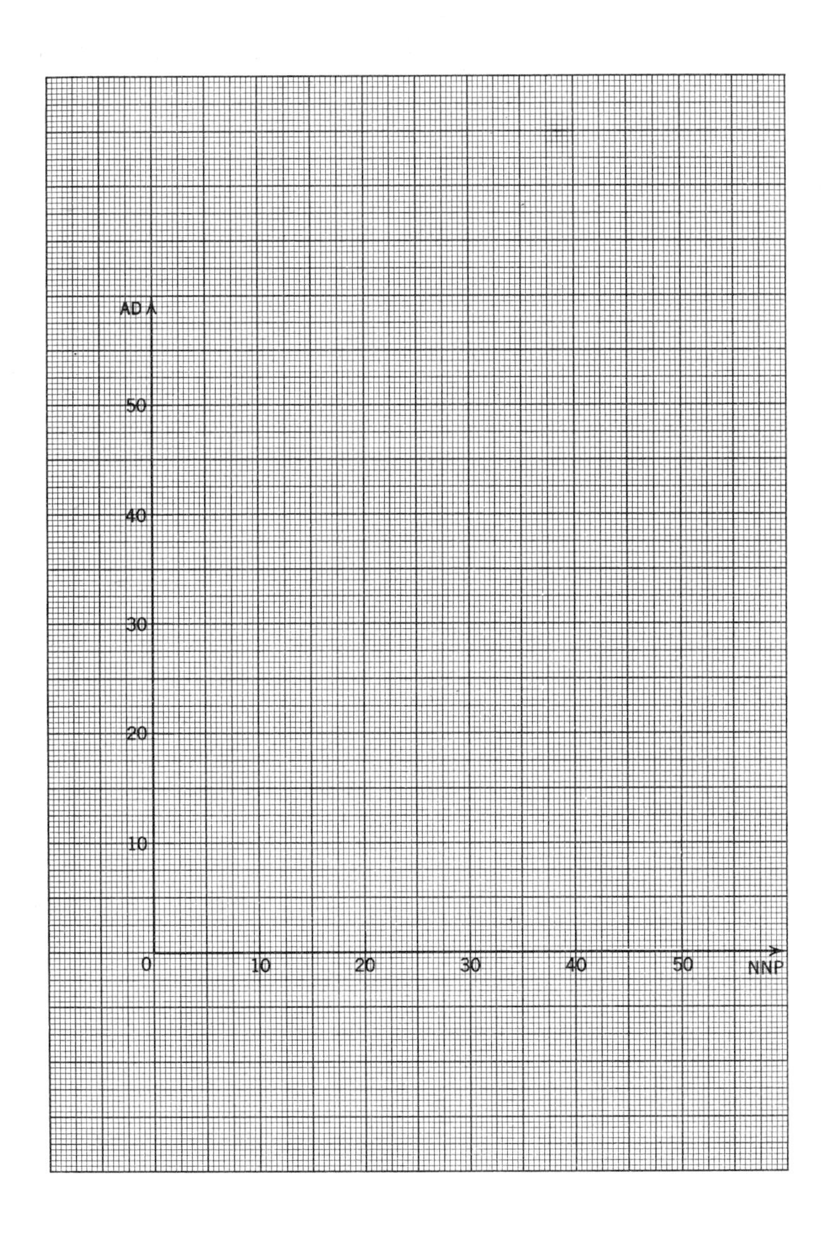
AD
50
40
30
20
10
0
10
20
30
40
50
NNP

VI. THE DIAGRAM OF SAVING AND INVESTMENT WITH THE GOVERNMENT INCLUDED

We were able to develop in Chapter 2 the analysis of the determination of equilibrium *NNP* with either of two diagrams: an *AD*-and-*AS* diagram or an *S*-and-*ID* diagram. We have now shown how government demand and taxation can be introduced into the *AD*-and-*AS* diagram; it remains to show how they can be introduced into the *S*-and-*ID* diagram.

We learned on page 91 that

$$NNP = C + NPS + NT. \qquad (5.4)$$

If we assume that households are able to buy all the goods and services that they are willing to pay for—there is no rationing except by price—then the amount consumed (C) will equal *CD*. We can, therefore write

$$NNP = CD + NPS + NT. \qquad (5.10)$$

Since equilibrium requires that *NNP* equal *AD*, and since *AD* is equal to the sum of *CD*, *ID*, and *GD*,

$$CD + ID + GD = NNP = CD + NPS + NT. \qquad (5.11)$$

Eliminating *CD* from both sides of this equation gives us another equilibrium condition; it is

$$ID + GD = NPS + NT. \qquad (5.12)$$

In Figure 5-4, *ID* plus *GD* and *NPS* plus *NT* are shown on the vertical axis and *NNP* on the horizontal. Since we are treating *ID* and *GD* as constants, their sum is a constant and is shown as a horizontal line. No matter what *NNP* is, *ID* plus *GD* is the same.

The other line is the saving-plus-tax function. It is found by adding *NT*, which are assumed constant, to *NPS* which would exist at each level of *NNP*. The relationship between the sum of *NT* and *NPS* and the *NNP* can be found from the *CD* function. Since

$$CD = (AC - mpcNT) + mpcNNP, \qquad (5.9)$$

and

$$NPS = NNP - CD - NT, \qquad (5.10)$$

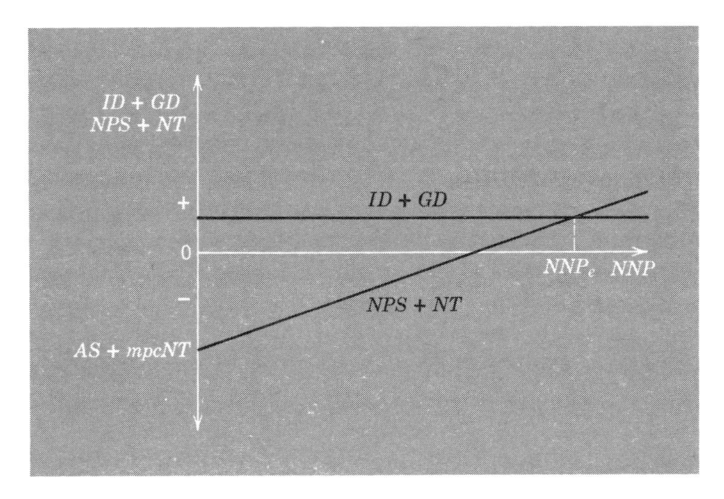

Figure 5-4

we find by eliminating *CD* from these two equations that

$$NT + NPS = -AC + mpcNT + (1 - mpc)\ NNP. \tag{5.13}$$

Since the marginal propensity to save (*mps*) is equal to 1 minus the *mpc* and *AC* is equal to the negative of autonomous saving (*AS*), this equation can be rewritten as

$$NT + NPS = (AS + mpcNT) + mpsNNP. \tag{5.14}$$

The slope of this function is the marginal propensity to save; its intercept is *AS* plus *NT* multiplied by the marginal propensity to consume.

Equilibrium *NNP* is found in Figure 5-4 at the level of *NNP* at which *NPS* plus *NT* is equal to *GD* plus *ID*. If *NNP* is greater than this, *AD* will be less than *NNP*; *NNP* will decrease. If the *NNP* is less than this, AD will be greater than the *NNP*; the *NNP* will rise.

An increase in *GD* will raise the *ID*-plus-*GD* line and raise the equilibrium level of *NNP* by a multiple of the increase in *GD*. The multiple depends on the slope of the *NPS*-plus-*NT* function, which is the marginal propensity to save.

A reduction in *NT* lowers the *NPS*-plus-*NT* function by the marginal propensity to consume times the tax reduction and increases the equilibrium *NNP*.

QUESTIONS

1. Assuming that *ACD* is \$15 billion, the *mpc* out of disposable income is 0.5, and *NT* are \$10 billion, carefully draw in the *NPS*-plus-*NT* function on the graph on the next page.
2. Assuming that *ID* is \$4 billion and *GD* is \$11 billion, draw the *ID*-plus-*GD* function on the same graph. What is equilibrium *NNP*?
3. Explain why, with reference to the diagram, a \$1 billion reduction in *NT* will increase equilibrium *NNP* by less than a \$1 billion increase in *GD*.

VII. THE ALGEBRA

Equilibrium *NNP* can be found algebraically by equating *ID* plus *GD* to *NPS* plus *NT* and solving for *NNP*. Since

$$NT + NPS = -AC + mpcNT + mps\,NNP, \qquad (5.13)$$

by equating *ID* plus *GD* to *NT* plus *NPS*, we find that

$$ID + GD = -AC + mpcNT + mpsNNP. \qquad (5.14)$$

Solving for *NNP*, we find that

$$NNP = \frac{1}{mps}(ID + AC) + \frac{1}{mps}GD - \frac{mpc}{mps}NT. \quad (5.15)$$

The coefficient of *GD* is $1/mps$ which tells us that a dollar increase in *GD* will raise equilibrium *NNP* by the reciprocal of the marginal propensity to save. Since the marginal propensity to save is a fraction, the *NNP* rises by a multiple of an increase in *GD*.

To discover the effect of a change in *NT* on *NNP* we must examine the coefficient of *NT* in the equation. It is the negative of mpc/mps. Although a cut in taxes raises equilibrium *NNP*, the increase will depend on the marginal propensity to consume; it need not be a multiple of the tax cut. If the marginal propensity to consume were less than 0.5, the *NNP* would rise by less than the tax cut. For example, if the marginal propensity to consume

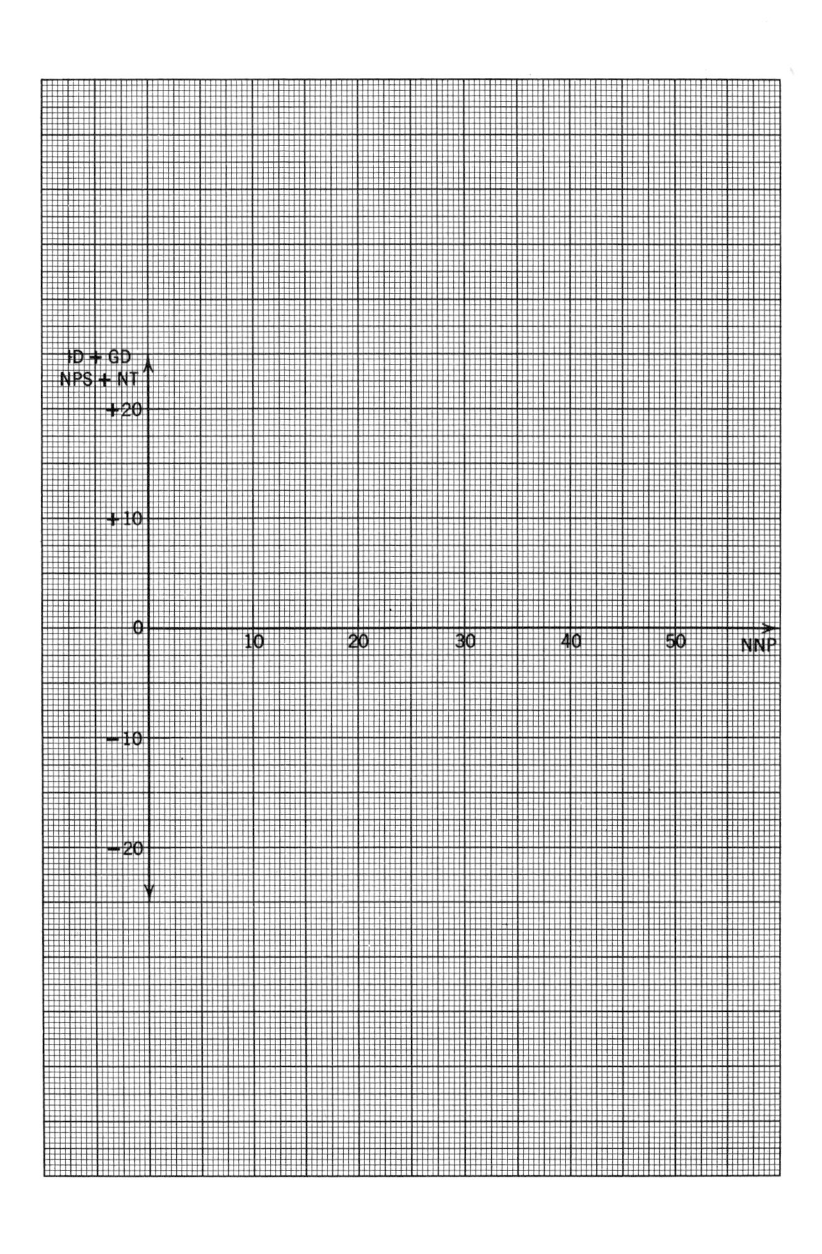
ID + GD
NPS + NT
+20
+10
0
−10
−20
10
20
30
40
50
NNP

is 0.4 then the *mps* is 0.6; a dollar cut in taxes would raise the *NNP* by two thirds of a dollar.

QUESTIONS

1. (a) Assuming that *ACD* is \$15 billion, the *mpc* out of *DY* is 0.5, *NT* are \$10 billion, *ID* is \$4 billion, and *GD* is \$11 billion, find equilibrium *NNP* algebraically.
   (b) Increase *GD* by \$1 billion. What happens to *NNP*?
   (c) Decrease *NT* by \$1 billion. What happens to *NNP*?
2. How would the answers to Question 1 change if the *mpc* were 0.9 rather than 0.5?

VIII. THE COMMON SENSE OF FISCAL POLICY

We have derived one result in three ways. An increase in demand by the government for buildings, roads, or labor raises the production of goods and services by a multiple amount; the multiple is equal to the reciprocal of the marginal propensity to save. A reduction in taxes also increases the NNP, but by a smaller amount than an equivalent increase in government demand. For each dollar reduction in taxes, output rises by the marginal propensity to consume divided by the marginal propensity to save.

This conclusion is of enormous importance. To make certain that it is understood, let us present a common-sense explanation. We know that business firms are not going to produce continually more than they can sell, nor can they chronically sell more than they produce. Consequently, there is a strong tendency for the total production of goods and services to equal aggregate demand. If a million pairs of shoes are demanded, a million pairs will be produced. Therefore, if the government demands more goods and services when the economy is operating at less than full employment, firms will increase their production to meet the increase in demand. Since income is equal to output, if the government has a road built, incomes in the forms of wages and salaries, rent, interest, and profits rise by the value of the road. And this increase in income induces a secondary increase in the demand by households for consumer goods and services. Constructing the road creates income, and part of that income is spent for food, clothing, entertainment, etc. The size of the secondary increase in demand depends on the amount of any increase in income that households tend to spend on consumer goods and services; it depends on the marginal propensity to consume. Since some of the increased income will be saved, the increased demand for food, clothing, and entertainment will be less than the increase in income.

When the demand for consumer goods and services increases, the producers of these things react by increasing their output. Therefore, output rises by more than just the value of the road. And we must not stop the analysis here, since the increased production of food, clothing, and entertainment implies an increase in wages and salaries, rent, interest, and profits for those who produce these goods and services. With additional income, households will increase their demand for consumer goods and services still further, and the NNP, employment, and income rise some more. And so it goes. Since the marginal propensity to consume is a fraction, each round of new demand is smaller than the last. Income will rise by some multiple of the increase in government demand. The community will end up, not only with a new road, but also with more food, clothing, entertainment, etc.

Consider a more specific example. If the government spent $1 million building a road, incomes of those who contributed to the production of the road would rise by $1 million. If the marginal propensity to consume were 0.8, then the households who received this income would spend $800,000 on consumer goods. The production of consumer goods would, therefore, rise by this amount, as producers satisfied the demand. The act of producing the consumer goods generates $800,000 of further income, for those who contributed to their production. Eight-tenths of this income would be consumed. Therefore, the demand for consumer goods would again increase; this time by $640,000. Manufacturers would expand their production by this amount to satisfy the demand and create $640,000 worth of income for those who contributed to the production. Eight-tenths of that income, $512,000, would appear as a further demand for consumer goods, creating more production and income. At this stage the original $1 million expenditure by the government has led to an increase in output of not just $1 million, but $2,952,000, that is, $1 million plus $800,000 plus $640,000 plus $512,000. And further income would be created. With the marginal propensity to consume equal to 0.8, the total increase in output would be $5 million. The community would end up with a road worth $1 million and $4 million more of consumer goods.

Now let us consider a change in taxes. A tax reduction does not itself increase aggregate demand, but it does raise disposable income. People have more take-home pay. The increase in disposable income increases the demand for consumer goods and services by an amount depending on the marginal propensity to consume. If taxes fall by $1 billion and if households spend on consumer goods and services seven-tenths of any increase in disposable income, then the demand for consumer goods will rise by $700 million. To meet this increase in demand, business firms will expand their production of the goods demanded, creating in the process $700 million worth of income for those who contributed to the production. A further increase in consumption demand would be induced by households having more disposable income. With the marginal propensity to consume equal to 0.7, the demand for consumer goods would rise by $490, leading to more production and more income. Each round of increased consumption demand gets smaller, since only a fraction of an increase in income is spent. In the example we have been considering, the total effect of a tax cut of $1 billion would be an increase in the NNP of $2⅓ billion.

IX. THE KEYNESIAN VERSUS THE CLASSICAL VIEW OF FISCAL POLICY

The conclusions reached thus far in this chapter are in conflict with much that the classical economists taught. The notion that the economy can be helped by reducing taxes or raising government demand, creating a deficit, has only recently become respectable. A classical economist would have argued that an increase in government demand, no matter how financed, would have no effect on total employment. Let us consider how they would have analyzed the repercussions of increased GD.

An increase in government spending can be financed in one of three ways: taxing, borrowing, or creating money. Let us consider GD financed by taxation first. According to Keynesian theory, an increase in GD financed by an increase in taxes raises the NNP; when the government taxes and spends a dollar, its demand rises by a dollar, but consumption demand falls by less than a dollar, since the marginal propensity to consume is a fraction. Classical economists, however, would have argued that an increase in GD financed by an increase in taxes had no effect at all on AD and, therefore, no effect on the NNP. Each dollar of taxation reduces private spending by a dollar, rather than a fraction of a dollar.

The classical economists could easily accept the notion of a fractional marginal propensity to consume and could agree that the reduction in DY resulting from the increase in taxes would lead only to a fractional reduction in consumption demand. But they would not have stopped there in their analysis. They would have gone on to argue that the taxes reduced saving as well, and these savings would also have been spent. If individual savers did not wish to buy buildings, equipment, or inventories with their savings, they would have lent them to someone who would have. If, for example, the marginal propensity to consume were 0.8, then an increase in taxes of $10 would reduce consumption demand by $8 and ID by $2; private demand would fall by $10. If the government spent $10, there would be no increase in AD.

Keynesian theory implies that an increase in GD financed by new taxes will raise the equilibrium NNP by exactly the amount of increased GD. Why is this true? Recall that the sum of *ID* and *GD* equals the sum of *NPS* and *NT* (Eq. 5.12). If *GD* and *NT* are increased by the same amount and if ID is constant, as we have assumed, then NPS must also be constant. Since NPS depends on DY, DY must be unchanged if NPS is to be unchanged. In the absence of business saving, DY is equal to the NNP minus NT. Since NT have increased and DY must not increase, the NNP must increase by the same amount as GD.

Consider an example. If GD and NT are increased by $100 million and if ID is unchanged, then NS is unchanged. NS depends on DY; therefore, DY is unchanged. DY is the difference between NNP and NT. Since NT are up $100 million, NNP must also be up $100 million.

This precise result, that the NNP will rise by the same amount as an increase in GD when the expenditure is financed out of taxation, should not be taken too seriously. If we were correct in the first chapter to argue that some saving generally does not lead to investment demand, then the qualitative result derived from the elementary version of Keynesian theory would be correct, although the quantitative one would not. When the government taxes and spends, spending will rise a bit, because some of the money that is taxed away would not have been spent. The amount not spent would be a fraction of the amount that would have been saved, not the amount that would have been saved. The classical conclusion differs from the Keynesian; it gives the wrong qualitative result, because the classical writers believed incorrectly that hoarding never occurred.

Now let us consider an increase in GD financed by the sale of bonds. Again the classical writers would have argued that the total demand for goods and services would be unaffected. The bonds of the government compete with other securities in the market for loanable funds, with the result that each dollar the government secures by selling bonds would have been lent to someone else who would have spent it. Government demand rises, but ID falls by exactly the same amount.

Keynesian theory implies that the NNP will rise by a multiple of any increase in GD financed by selling bonds. When we considered an increase in GD earlier in this chapter, we assumed that ID was unchanged. We must now admit that this is an exaggeration. The competition of the government for credit would raise the cost of credit and reduce its availability; ID would decline.

Although we again see that the quantitative result derived from Keynesian theory is not right, it does give the correct qualitative result. Investment demand can be expected to fall as a result of the tightening of credit, but by less than the increase in GD. As interest rates rise and credit becomes scarcer, individuals and firms economize on their use of money; money that would have been inactive becomes active and spending rises. Again it would seem that Keynes theory and classical theory give different results, because the classical analysis does not allow for hoarding and dishoarding. The competition of the government for funds will lead to dishoarding and, therefore, an increase in AD and the NNP, as Keynesian theory implies.

Finally, we must consider an increase in GD or reduction in NT financed by the creation of new money. The new money may be pieces of paper printed by the U.S. Treasury or bank deposits that did not exist before. Classical and Keynesian theories agree on one consequence of this action; AD rises. But the agreement goes no further. According to classical writers, the increase in AD would simply lead to an increase in prices. In their view, as we explained in Chapter 1, AD is always equal to full-employment NNP. Any increase in AD can lead only to excess demand and inflation.

Keynesian theory assumes that wages and prices are rigid downward, which eliminates any presumption that the economy will operate at full employment. An increase in GD financed by the creation of money need not lead to significant price increases, but rather could lead to a multiple increase in the NNP, as the analysis in the earlier sections of this chapter has shown. The total effect on the NNP could very well be greater than the change in GD times the reciprocal of the marginal propensity to save. As NNP rises, NPS will increase. Some of this saving will result in greater ID; it will not all be hoarded. NNP will rise even further.

QUESTIONS

1. Assume that GD and NT rise by $10.

    (a) Explain why the version of Keynesian theory presented in this chapter implies that the NNP will rise by $10.

    (b) Explain why classical analysis implies that AD will be unchanged.

    (c) If an expansion of the NNP pushes up interest rates, explain why the NNP will rise by less than $10.

2. Assume that the government sells $10 worth of bonds and spends the money on goods and services.

    (a) Explain why the elementary version of Keynesian theory implies that the NNP will rise by $10 divided by the mps.

    (b) Explain why classical theory implies that AD and the NNP will be unchanged.

    (c) If the cost and availability of credit affect ID, explain why the NNP would rise, but by less than $10 divided by the marginal propensity to save.

3. Assume that GD rises by $10 and that the government prints money to pay for the increased expenditure.

(a) Explain why Keynesian theory implies that the NNP will rise by $10 divided by mps.

(b) Explain why classical analysis implies that the only consequence will be a rise in prices.

(c) Assuming that the cost and availability of credit affect ID, explain why the NNP will rise by more than $10 divided by mps.

X. DEFICIT SPENDING AND THE NATIONAL DEBT

To many people, deficit spending and the national debt are closely associated. Increasing government demand or reducing taxes in order to maintain full employment seems to imply a growing national debt. Since a growing national debt seems bad, many are not at all certain that the government should unbalance its budget in order to achieve full employment. Even if they agree that the government could achieve this objective, they reject the policy because they believe the cost is too great.

It is desirable, therefore, that we consider some questions about the national debt. What is it? How is it created? In what sense is it a disadvantage? Is it a burden on future generations? Does a fiscal policy aimed at the maintenance of full employment imply a growing national debt?

By the national debt is usually meant the total value of the interest-bearing obligations of the United States Government held outside the government. There are two reasons why one might be concerned about it. First, one may believe that one day the government will have to pay off the national debt; second, because the government has to pay interest to holders of the debt.

The first concern is purely imaginary. The United States Government does what most businessmen do when their debt matures; it contracts new debt. When bonds must be paid off, new bonds are issued to pay off the holders of the old ones. Although it may be *desirable* to reduce the national debt, it is not *necessary* to do so. So long as the government has the ability to meet its financial obligations, it can always sell new bonds when old bonds mature. Since the United States Government can create money if it has to, there can be no question of its ability to meet its financial obligations. Thus, the national debt need not ever be paid off.

Although the national debt can always be with us, there is the requirement that the government pay interest to its holders. It is often maintained that this is undesirable, because it places a burden on future generations which will be forced to pay interest on debt contracted by their forebears. Although it may be true that a growing national debt implies higher taxes to pay interest in the future, it is often overlooked that future generations will be paying the interest to themselves. If a national debt is held within the country, internally, future generations will also be recipients of the interest, because they will be holding the bonds. The existence of the debt should not make anyone sorry for some abstract average American yet unborn, since he will inherit the bonds that will receive the interest. Individuals who inherit no assets from their parents will have to pay interest without receiving any, while individuals who inherit great wealth will receive more interest than they pay. But if one talks about the future generation as a whole, it will receive and pay the interest; it will pay it to itself.

It does not follow that there is no burden associated with the debt. If incentives depend on income after taxes and if the payment of interest on the debt requires taxes, incentives may be reduced. If one believes that future generations are going to be induced to work less hard because of taxation to pay interest on the national debt, then one may legitimately worry about the burden on future Americans resulting from the existence of an internally held debt.

We can admit that the national debt is a burden without concluding that deficit spending implies a growing national debt. If the government believed that any existing nonfrictional unemployment could be eliminated by an increase in aggregate demand, it could increase its demand for goods and services or reduce taxes without increasing the national debt. If the budget were balanced initially, it would be true that the increase in GD or reduction in NT would lead to a deficit which had to be financed some way, but it would not follow that the national debt need grow. The deficit could be financed by creating money.

A classical economist would have argued that printing money would be inflationary, but he would have been implicitly assuming that the economy already had enough aggregate demand to maintain full employment. But when aggregate demand is deficient, the classical analysis is simply inapplicable. Although the government could print currency and spend it to finance the deficit, this would be unlikely in our economy. If new currency were printed, the government would in all probability give it to the Federal Reserve Banks in exchange for demand deposits and then use these deposits to pay for its expenditures.

A slight complication is introduced if the Treasury hesitates to print more currency or if the Congress does not allow this method of finance. But it still does not follow that the national debt must grow. The Treasury could then sell bonds to the Federal Reserve Banks to obtain the deposits that it needs to finance its deficit. Although one might think that this implies an increase in the national debt, since the Federal Reserve Banks would have more government securities, there would actually be no meaningful increase in the national debt.

The Federal Reserve Banks are permitted to pay their member bank stockholders a 6% return on the original amounts contributed to establish the Federal Reserve Banks. If the Federal Reserve Banks are more profitable than this, and they are, all excess profits are paid to the Treasury. Under present circumstances, therefore, any increase in Fed holdings of government securities results in the Treasury's paying them interest, which is then returned to the Treasury. If the Treasury issued new currency, giving it to the Federal Reserve Banks for deposits, it would have to pay no interest in the future. But it is equally true that if it gave the Federal Reserve Banks interest-bearing securities, it would still not have to pay any future interest. If the rate of interest is 5% on government securities, an increase in Fed holdings of government securities of $2 billion will increase Treasury payments to the Federal Reserve Banks by $100 million a year. But the banks would then return this money to the Treasury. In either case it comes to the same thing, whether cash or bonds are given to the Fed for the deposits that are needed to finance a deficit.

There is a tradition and there are rules preventing the Treasury from selling securities *directly* to the Federal Reserve Banks. Although this would seem to imply that the government must increase the national debt to finance a deficit if unable or unwilling to create money to pay for it, this is not so. Imagine that the Treasury is forced by Congress to finance a deficit by selling bonds on the open market. Will the national debt then increase?

If the Treasury believes that a $10 billion cut in taxes, financed by printing money, is sufficient to achieve full employment and if it sells $10 billion worth of securities to the public to permit the tax reduction, then the NNP would increase, but the increase would be less than is necessary to have full employment. If a $10 billion tax cut, financed by new money, is just enough to achieve full employment, then the same tax cut, financed by selling bonds, is not enough. In the latter case, there is a competition for funds in the market which would tend to raise interest rates and reduce the availability of credit; investment demand would fall. If, in spite of the apparent inadequacy of a $10 billion tax cut financed by the sale of bonds, the Treasury did not make the tax cut larger, aggregate demand would be insufficient to promote full employment. The economy would have more employment, but still less than full employment, and it would appear that the national debt would grow.

But the full story is not told. The Federal Reserve authorities also have a responsibility for maintaining full employment. If their assessment of the current economic situation coincides with that of the Congress and Treasury, they would be obliged to engage in open-market purchases of government securities to reduce the cost of credit and to increase its availability. The Federal Reserve Banks would buy the securities that the Treasury sold.

Be careful to note that there need be no agreement between the Federal Reserve authorities and the Treasury that the Fed will buy the securities. If they assess the economic situation similarly, they will agree as to how much aggregate demand is necessary to achieve full employment. If they both pursue that goal, the Federal Reserve will automatically finance any Treasury deficit created in order to achieve full employment. With the new bonds winding up in the hands of the Federal Reserve Banks, the Treasury will be paying interest only to have it returned. There will be no burden on such a debt.

Nothing that has been said here should be interpreted to imply that there is never any reason for a growing national debt. All we have maintained is that pursuit of the goal of full employment need not imply a growing debt. If aggregate demand were excessive for any reason, the monetary authorities might sell bonds to increase the cost and reduce the availability of credit. Then the bonds in the possession of the public would rise, and the Treasury would have to pay more interest; interest that used to return to the Treasury would no longer do so. We can sum up this section by saying that the national debt is created to control excessive aggregate demand not to promote sufficient demand. Deficient aggregate demand can be eliminated without increasing the national debt.

QUESTIONS

1. Can an American business firm stay permanently in debt?
2. If a national debt is internally held, who in the future is going to receive the interest payments?
3. Why may the need to pay interest on the national debt reduce incentives?
4. Why is not paper money, issued by the Treasury, included in the national debt?
5. Why should government securities held by the Federal Reserve Banks be excluded from the National Debt?
6. If the Treasury can and will print money, why does not a deficit created to achieve full employment imply a growing national debt?
7. If the Treasury can sell bonds to the Federal Reserve Banks, why does not a deficit created to achieve full employment imply a growing national debt?
8. If the Treasury cannot print money or sell bonds directly to the Federal Reserve Banks, why does not a deficit created to achieve full employment imply a growing national debt? Assume that the Federal Reserve authorities assess the current economic situation in exactly the same manner as the Administration and Congress.

XI. A FINAL COMMENT

Some people react to the ideas that have been presented in this chapter with skepticism. Although the arguments appear valid, it all seems too easy. They wonder why, if a depression can be cured by increased government spending or reduced taxes without even an increase in the national debt, the Great Depression of the 1930s was not ended this way. Surely if the cure is obvious to us, they feel, it would have been obvious to everyone then.

But something may be obvious after it has been pointed out, although not obvious previously. If someone had asked economic theorists in the 1930s if unemployment was possible if wages and prices were rigidly downward, they would probably have answered yes. If they were then asked if increased government demand for goods and services or reduced taxes, financed by the creation of money, would eliminate that unemployment, they might also have answered yes after they had a chance to think about it. Except for Keynes and a few others, the questions were not being asked. Economists and politicians still seemed to believe that there was an inherent mechanism in the economy that would generate full employment and that deficit spending would lead to inflation.

Creating money to increase government demand would be inflationary if the economy were operating at full employment. What was not understood in the 1930s was that, when the economy was operating at less than full employment, an increase in aggregate demand would raise the real NNP and employment; it did not simply lead to inflation.

In order to understand the faulty reasoning that led men to apply statements valid at full employment to situations of less than full employment, consider the following analogy. Imagine that some doctor long ago wondered whether a blood transfusion could make a man healthier. If he tried to discover the answer by giving a pint of blood to a healthy man, he would undoubtedly have concluded that it did him no good. If he increased the dose to a quart he would have found that the man was harmed and that when the blood transfusion was very great, the blood being forced into the healthy man, it would cause his death. If the doctor concluded that a small blood transfusion never did any good and that a large blood transfusion was disastrous, he would have been wrong.

If a *healthy* man is given more blood, no good can come of it, and, if he is given enough, he can only be harmed, possibly fatally if the amount of blood is too great. But that a blood transfusion is never desirable is a false inference, since we know that when a man does not have sufficient blood, his life can be saved by one.

It was just this kind of false inference that was responsible for the widely held view that an increase in the money supply would never help the economy and could only cause injury. The conceptual experiment that led to this conclusion was conducted on a healthy economy; one in which the aggregate demand for goods and services always equaled full-employment NNP. The conclusion is correct for such an economy, but it is not correct for an economy in which aggregate demand is less than full-employment NNP. Then the economy can be aided by an infusion of new money in the same sense that a person lacking sufficient blood can be helped by an infusion of new blood.

QUESTIONS

1. If a mature man needs 3000 calories to maintain his ideal weight, what happens to him if he consumes more than 3000 calories a day?
2. Why would it be wrong to conclude that consuming more than 3000 calories a day necessarily raises a man's weight above the ideal? Consider someone who is below his ideal weight and someone who is growing.
3. (a) If an economy were not growing and if it had just enough demand to buy all that could be produced at full employment at present prices, what would happen if the money supply increased?

   (b) Why would it be wrong to conclude that an increase in the money supply necessarily has this result? Consider an economy that has insufficient demand and one that is growing.

XII. SUMMARY

1. When we allow for the existence of government, the statement of the net national product is altered from what it was in Chapter 2. Government expenditures must be added to consumption and to NPDI on the left side of the statement; indirect business taxes must be added to the right.

2. When government and foreign trade is ignored, NPDI is necessarily equal to NPS. Introduction of government alters this identity. It then becomes NPDI plus G equals NPS plus NT.

3. Equilibrium NNP depends in part on government demand and net taxes. There are three ways that the Keynesian theory of the determination of the NNP can be presented. First, the AD and AS functions can be drawn. AD consists of ID, GD, and CD. CD is a function of DY. DY differs from NNP by NT, if business saving is assumed to be zero. Second, a S-plus-T and an ID-plus-GD diagram can be used. Taxes, investment demand, and government demand are treated as constants, S is assumed to depend on

DY, and, with NT assumed constant, on the NNP. Equilibrium NNP is found at the point at which S plus T equals ID plus GD. Finally, the CD function can be written as an equation, and equilibrium NNP can be found algebraically.

4. All methods must yield the same result. The theory implies that an increase in GD raises the NNP by the change in GD times the reciprocal of the marginal propensity to save. A reduction in taxes raises the NNP by the change in taxes times the ratio of the marginal propensity to consume to the marginal propensity to save.

5. Classical economists arrived at different conclusions concerning the effects of increased GD or reduced taxes. An increase in GD, financed by either taxes or bond sales, would have no effect on AD, according to their analysis. They believed that all funds collected would have been spent anyway, so that no increase in demand occurs. Keynesian theory assumes that ID is unaffected by a reduction in saving or an increase in competition for funds in the money markets. Under most circumstances this would not be true. Some saving would lead to investment demand and some investment demand may fail to appear if the cost of credit increases. The Keynesian theory does give the right qualitative answer, however, while the classical theory does not. Some saving does not lead to investment demand, and the government can therefore withdraw some money from the lendable funds market without reducing the funds available to others by that amount. Higher interest rates encourage people to lend, and money that would not have been in circulation is lent and spent.

6. Classical economists believed that an increase in GD, financed by printing money, would lead to price inflation. They assumed that the economy was always operating at full employment and any increase in demand would make AD excessive. But, if the economy is operating at less than full employment, and sometimes it is, an increase in GD, financed by creating money, raises the NNP by a multiple.

7. The national debt includes all interest-bearing securities issued by the national government and held outside the government. It does not have to be paid off at any time in the future. Our government can do what many corporations do, issue new bonds when the old ones mature. Interest must be paid on the

debt, however, and some people feel that this is a burden on future generations. But future generations will not only have to pay the interest, they will also receive the interest. There is a sense in which this could be a burden if the taxes that they pay to finance the interest reduce their incentives.

8. Whether the national debt is a burden or not, a full-employment policy need not imply a growing national debt. If the government decides to maintain AD by raising its demand or by cutting taxes, it can finance its deficit by creating money. If the Congress does not permit this method of finance, it can sell bonds to the Federal Reserve Banks and this will not imply a growing debt, since the interest received by the Federal Reserve Banks will return to the Treasury. If the Congress does not permit the Treasury to sell bonds directly to the Federal Reserve Banks, the same result follows if the Banks buy bonds as the Treasury sells them. This could occur without any agreement between the Treasury and the Fed to buy the bonds sold by the Treasury. If the Federal Reserve authorities assess the current economic situation in the same way as the Treasury and Congress, they would automatically buy bonds as the Treasury sells them.

9. Keynesian theory teaches us that depressions because of insufficient demand need not persist. Policy conclusions based on a classical analysis that assumes full employment should not prevent us from advocating deficits when there is less than full employment.

6

Identifying the Causes of Unemployment and Inflation

The primary objectives of this book have been to explain how nonfrictional unemployment can occur, and when it does, how it can be remedied. In the process of developing the analysis, we have also given an explanation of inflation; when aggregate demand exceeds full-employment NNP, prices rise and inflation occurs. We have emphasized, however, that an increase in aggregate demand is not necessarily inflationary. Until full employment is reached, an increase in demand can raise output and employment without having a significant effect on wages and prices. According to this analysis, full employment without inflation is an achievable objective. For if prices are rising, demand must be excessive and can be reduced without causing unemployment. If nonfrictional unemployment exists, aggregate demand can be increased and unemployment eliminated without generating inflation.

Unfortunately this may be an oversimplification of reality. Full employment and price stability may be more difficult to achieve. For one thing, we can never be certain about the extent of frictional unemployment and cannot therefore know if we are experiencing nonfrictional unemployment. Unemployment cannot be prevented if it cannot be identified. Furthermore, price stability and full employment may be incompatible objectives. If they are incompatible, one must be sacrificed to achieve the other. These are troublesome problems, and we now turn to their consideration.

I. THE MAGNITUDE OF FRICTIONAL UNEMPLOYMENT

If we were living in a stationary state without any change occurring in the economy, frictional unemployment would not exist. But in reality, changes in demand and supply occur constantly in almost all markets. Other factors being constant, the more change the more frictional unemployment there will be. Since economic change does not take place at an even rate, there is no reason to believe that frictional unemployment will be a specific percentage of the labor force. This makes the formation of sound economic policy difficult.

If the extent of change in the economy always caused 3% of the labor force to be unemployed, a deficiency of aggregate demand could be discovered simply by looking at unemployment statistics, assuming, of course, that they were accurate. If the percentage of the labor force unemployed rose above 3%, we would know that there was nonfrictional unemployment, and monetary and fiscal actions could be taken to eliminate it. But when we do not know the percentage of the labor force frictionally unemployed, we cannot tell from unemployment statistics whether more aggregate demand is called for. Last year, frictional unemployment may have been 3%, but this year it is 5%. A 5% unemployment rate last year would have called for easy money or deficit spending, whereas the same rate this year would call for neither policy; more aggregate demand would only lead to inflation.

Since there is no easy way to calculate frictional unemployment, reasonable men may disagree over the monetary and fiscal policies that are currently required. Those who believe that frictional unemployment can be as high as 5% may advocate fiscal and monetary restraint, while those who believe that frictional unemployment does not usually run this high may be advocating fiscal and monetary ease. Both groups may believe that aggregate demand can and should be regulated by government, but disagree whether it is sufficient at present. If the monetary authorities are especially sensitive to the dangers of inflation, they may tolerate a degree of unemployment that will horrify and enrage others. Before they take any action to stimulate demand they would want to be almost certain that it would not be inflationary. If, on the other hand, they are especially sensitive to the social consequences of unemployment, they may constantly overstimulate the economy and produce inflation.

QUESTIONS

1. What determines the percentage of the labor force that is frictionally unemployed?
2. Why cannot we assume that when there is more than 4% of the labor force unemployed, there is nonfrictional unemployment?
3. If the Federal Reserve authorities always kept interest rates relatively high unless they were certain that there was nonfrictional unemployment, why would they be criticized by some?
4. If the Federal Reserve authorities always kept interest rates relatively low unless they were certain that there was no nonfrictional unemployment, why would they be criticized by some?

II. COST-PUSH INFLATION

Some economic observers believe that the United States economy experienced a new phenomenon in 1958: rising prices and nonfrictional unemployment at the same time. Although standard inflation theory holds that prices rise only when demand exceeds full-employment output, it appeared that output could be below that level and yet prices could rise. A new explanation of inflation seemed called for, and one was offered. It suggested that monopoly power was responsible for inflation. This new kind of inflation has been given many names, among them, wage, cost-push, and seller's inflation.

It is not certain that the economy did, in fact, experience any new phenomenon. Since our indices of prices and unemployment are imperfect and since we cannot determine precisely how much unemployment is of the frictional type, a person who strongly believed that the only cause of inflation was excessive aggregate demand might be unconvinced by the evidence. But cost-push inflation, nonetheless, cannot be dismissed as an impossibility.

If wages and prices are inflexible downward because of imperfections of competition, the same imperfections could lead to wage and price increases without excessive aggregate demand. In a highly competitive economy, wages fall when there are more people looking for work than there are jobs available, and in such an economy prices fall when there is excess capacity. But if unions can prevent wage reductions, even though there is unemployment, and business firms can prevent price reductions, even though they have excess capacity, a supply-and-demand explanation of wages and prices is not possible. If unions have monopoly power, what is to prevent them from demanding and sometimes getting wage increases in spite of unemployment? If business firms have monopoly power, what is to prevent them from raising their prices in spite of excess capacity? In an imperfectly competitive economy, cost-push inflation is certainly a possibility.

QUESTIONS

1. If the labor and commodity markets were highly competitive, what would happen to wages and prices if there were nonfrictional unemployment and excess capacity?
2. If the labor and commodity markets are imperfectly competitive, could wages and prices rise, even though there were nonfrictional unemployment and excess capacity?

III. IDENTIFYING COST-PUSH INFLATION

Granted that cost-push inflation is a possibility, how can we decide if we are experiencing it? How can we determine whether an inflation is caused by excessive aggregate demand or monopoly power? Two tests have been offered. One suggests that we distinguish the two types of inflation by examining the rate of unemployment. The other holds that we must see which went up first, wages or prices.

According to the unemployment test, inflation that occurs when unemployment is relatively low is due to excess demand, whereas inflation that occurs when unemployment is relatively high is due to cost-push. But we have argued previously that no rate of unemployment can be used as a norm. If demand is excessive at the same time that rapid change is occurring, inflation and a relatively high unemployment rate can occur simultaneously. This test would be usable only if the quantity of frictional unemployment were known, but this may not be easy to determine.

Let us consider the other test; which went up first wages or prices? This test presumes, of course, that wage-push is responsible for the new kind of inflation, when and if it occurs. While excessive aggregate demand would be expected by some to raise prices before wages, this would also happen if price increases were caused by business firms simply raising prices, even though demand and cost conditions did not warrant it. But granting the premise that cost-push inflation is really wage-push inflation, this test would still have a fatal weakness.

If wages are observed to rise before prices, it does not follow that inflation is of the cost-push variety. Imagine that the economy is operating at full employment and that an increase in aggregate demand occurs. Business firms may not immediately raise prices; their first reaction may be to try to expand production. But with labor fully employed, this is not possible; if one firm expands, some other firm must contract. In their eagerness to secure more factors of production, firms would be more generous when labor contracts were renewed. Each firm would wish to hold its present labor force and even add to it. Wages would rise. The increase in wages would then lead firms to raise their prices, using increased costs as the justification for their actions. Although wages rose first and management could honestly argue that they increased their prices only because of the wage rise, this would not be an inflation of the cost-push variety. It would have been caused by excessive aggregate demand.

QUESTIONS

1. If prices rose with 4.5% of the labor force unemployed, why might some argue that inflation was due to cost-push? Why might they be wrong?
2. Why cannot you tell whether an inflation is due to cost-push or excess demand by seeing which went up first, wages or prices?

IV. COST-PUSH INFLATION AND A POLICY DILEMMA

Even if cost-push inflation could be identified, it is not clear that it could be controlled without creating an intolerable amount of unemployment. Cost-push inflation could, therefore, present a real dilemma to those responsible for controlling the economy.

If inflation and nonfrictional unemployment occurred simultaneously, the unemployment would suggest easy monetary and fiscal policy, while the inflation would call for restraint. If restraint were followed, unemployment would grow. If ease were pursued, unemployment would fall, but the authorities would be accused of fomenting inflation. And, in fact, they might be doing just that.

The greater the extent of unemployment, the more difficult it would be for unions to raise wages. And the greater the degree of excess capacity, the more difficult it would be for business firms to raise prices. Competition from the unemployed and competition between firms could become greater as unemployment and excess capacity grew. Thus, the monetary authorities could check excessive demands for higher wages and higher prices by making unemployment and excess capacity sufficiently great. Inflation is prevented not by eliminating excess demand but by making aggregate demand less than sufficient to maintain full employment. What an unpleasant outlook!

To some the alternative is clearly to be chosen, if a choice must be made. They will argue that a slow rate of increase of prices, creeping inflation, is not such a great evil; at least it is not as bad as unemployment. And by persisting, inflation will be anticipated; the unfair redistributive effects would, therefore, be slight.

There is a difficulty, however, with this argument. If a creeping inflation occurs because of excessive wage demands and if it fails to redistribute income toward wage receivers, the creep could become a gallop. Assume, for example, that unions insist on 5% wage increases when price stability would only allow a 4% increase. For a while prices could lag behind wage increases and unions could improve their relative share of income. But if the excessive wage demands of unions produced a rise of 1% a year in the price level and if this increase became generally expected, interest rates and prices would tend to rise today in anticipation of inflation tomorrow.

Higher interest rates and higher prices without proportionately higher wages would take away labor's gain of a 5% rather than a 4% increase in wages. If unions felt they were entitled to a 5% increase in real wages, they would no longer be getting that.

They might then insist on a 6% increase in money wages. When that happens, a 2% inflation could become expected, and the rate of increase of real wages could return to the 4% level. Then unions might insist on a 7% increase in wages. Or if they anticipate that the rate of increase of prices will rise, and that is just what has been happening, they might insist on an 8% or even a higher rate of increase of wages. And so it goes. Not only would prices rise forever, but the percentage rate of increase of prices would also grow. The creep could become a gallop. What another unpleasant prospect!

QUESTIONS

1. What are the objections to treating cost-push inflation by reducing aggregate demand?
2. What are the objections to maintaining aggregate demand equal to full-employment NNP, if cost-push inflation is occurring?

V. TREATING COST-PUSH INFLATION

A solution to this dilemma has been suggested. This is to keep wage increases in line with gains in productivity. The fundamental premise behind this idea is that if wages are tied to productivity, increases in wages will not require increases in prices; cost-push inflation would not occur.

To keep wage increases in line with gains in productivity, we must be able to measure changes in productivity. How can these be measured? The usual method of measuring labor productivity is to divide output by the number of workers. Productivity is defined to be the average output per man. There are two distinct reasons why such a number can increase. First, labor may become genuinely more productive in the sense that it can, working with the same amount of capital and other resources, produce more. Second, output per man may rise simply because machines are substituted for labor. This latter situation occurs, for example, when a firm automates; the same output takes less direct labor than previously. Although the average output of labor rises, there is no change in the inherent productivity of labor.

We must decide the type of change in the productivity of labor to which wages are to be related. The second possibility can be dismissed most easily. If a firm automates to such a degree that it needs only one worker where it previously used 1000, no one could seriously argue that the worker who remains should have his wages increased a thousandfold. It must therefore be productivity changes of the first variety that are meant to determine wage increases.

Although changes owing to an improvement in the inherent productive powers of labor might seem to justify the tying of wages to productivity, it would be difficult, if not impossible, to estimate the magnitude of such changes. If firms are adding new and better capital, how can one decide how much increased output per man to attribute to this factor and how much to an improvement in the inherent productivity of labor? Even if this problem were soluble, and changes in the inherent productive powers of labor could be determined, there is no natural law that dictates wage increases in line with such changes.

Imagine a self-sufficient farmer who produces directly for his own consumption. If he were to learn how to produce more with the same resources, his output would rise and he would be genuinely more productive. His living standard would improve in direct proportion to the improvement in his productivity. But what is true for the self-sufficient farmer is not necessarily true for someone living in a complex economy. If a farmer who is producing for the market becomes genuinely more productive, it does not follow that his income will rise. Unless he has a monopoly on improved methods, other farmers will also become more productive. The increase in output would depress the price and if demand were inelastic, all farmers would earn less, not more. The gains in productivity are passed on to the rest of the community. Only when some farmers switch to other activities would the remaining farmers share in the benefits that have come about because of their increased productivity.

Of course, if one really believed in this doctrine, one might insist that the government should, through some device like buying and storing agricultural commodities, see to it that farm incomes did rise in line with changes in productivity in agriculture. But imagine the consequences. There would be no incentive to leave agriculture. In fact, if productivity changes were relatively great in agriculture, instead of getting fewer farmers, we would have more, since their incomes would be rising the fastest. Without further governmental controls, the problem of agricultural surpluses would be truly enormous.

If the policy of rewarding labor in proportion to its inherent productivity were taken seriously, it would also imply that wages should never change in industries where there were no changes in productivity. But there are activities in our economy in which productivity changes are inherently slow, if they exist at all. For example, it is not clear that any productivity changes would be possible without a deterioration of quality in teaching, medicine, or haircutting. If teachers, doctors, and barbers are not to share in the growth in real incomes, who is to teach, who is to heal the sick, and who is to cut hair? Everyone would seek the jobs where productivity changes were the greatest, if the rule under consideration were followed. In a market economy not only is there no reason why factors of production should receive wage increases directly proportional to changes in their inherent productivity; there are also good reasons why this should not happen.

But there is an alternative meaning to the doctrine that wage increases should be kept in line with productivity changes. It is that *all* wages should rise at the rate of growth of labor productivity *in general.* It is changes in the ratio of the NNP to total employment that should set the limit to wage rates. If output per unit of labor increases at the rate of 4% per annum in the economy as a whole, then all wages should rise by 4% per year. Barbers, teachers, and doctors would then share in the growth of income, even though their productivity did not increase. This is the policy that many believe could prevent cost-push inflation.

If this rule were rigidly followed, relative wages would never change. If a machinist earned 25% more than a sweeper, this would be the case forever. But relative wages should reflect relative scarcity of various types of labor and should change in a well-functioning economy. When a particular type of labor becomes relatively scarce, it should enjoy a faster rate of increase of wages.

Even if the rule made sense, there would be extreme difficulty in getting unions to accept it. Those who are earning relatively little today are certain to feel that their wages should rise faster than the average. If they believed that their current wage was inequitable, they would not accept the notion that it should always remain at the same relative level. Their unions, if they have unions, would fight for wage increases greater than the average increase in productivity. Such wage increases might not cause inflation, if it could be determined whose wages were relatively too high to begin with, and therefore could increase at a slower rate. But if there are workers who are currently earning wages that are unjustifiably high, they are likely to have a strong union. Can we seriously expect a union in a strong bargaining position to seek wage increases less than the national average? Even if the union officers accepted the stronger goal of wage increases equal to the national average, they would be in danger of early replacement by more aggressive leaders.

QUESTIONS

1. How is the productivity of labor usually determined?
2. Give two reasons why labor productivity can rise.
3. If bricklayers suddenly began laying twice as many bricks per hour, would their wage increase in a competitive economy?
4. Are there groups in our economy who believe that they are relatively underpaid? Are there groups who believe that they are overpaid?
5. What do your answers to Question 4 imply about the prospects of labor being satisfied with wage increases equal to the average improvement in productivity in the whole economy?

VI. SUMMARY

1. In earlier chapters it was implied that full employment and price stability were compatible objectives. But, in reality, it is possible that neither objective can be achieved exactly, or one may have to be sacrificed to achieve the other.

2. The magnitude of frictional unemployment depends on the extent of change in the economy. The more change, the more frictional unemployment there will be. Since the degree of change is not always the same, there is no reason to expect that frictional unemployment will be a constant percentage of the

labor force. Since the magnitude of nonfrictional unemployment cannot be determined from unemployment statistics alone, there will be disagreement about whether more or less aggregate demand is desirable. Full employment may not be attainable because we cannot tell when we have it.

3. Some people believe that the American economy is the victim of a new problem: cost-push inflation. If wages and prices do not fall in the face of unemployment and excess capacity, they could rise under the same circumstances.

4. Although cost-push inflation is a possibility, it would be difficult to decide whether inflations were caused by excessive demand or cost-push. Although some have suggested that cost-push inflation exists when the rate of unemployment is more than 3% or 4%, the degree of frictional unemployment could lie outside of this range. Another test has, therefore, been suggested; see which went up first, wages or prices. The assumption is that cost-push inflation occurs when wages rise first. But an increase in demand for goods and services could lead to wage increases as firms bid more aggressively for labor, prior to any increase in prices; prices might rise only after wages have risen. It would not be possible, therefore, to conclude that cost-push inflation was occurring simply because wages seem to have risen prior to increases in prices.

5. Cost-push inflation would present a real dilemma to policy makers. To fight inflation, they should contract demand. But this might lead to unemployment, since the inflation is not due to excessive aggregate demand. A choice would have to be made, and it could not please everyone.

6. To prevent cost-push inflation, it has been suggested that wage increases be kept in line with productivity changes. There are various possible interpretations of this notion. One is that wages in a firm or industry should rise in line with output per man in that firm or industry, no matter what the reason for the increase. But if output per man rises simply because machines are substituted for labor in a firm, there is no rationale for advocating proportionately higher wages. Another interpretation is that wages should rise in a firm or industry directly in line with increases in the inherent productivity of labor in that firm or industry. Aside from the impossibility of determining such

changes in productivity, this notion is objectionable. In a market economy it does not follow that returns to factors of production rise with gains in productivity; they could even fall. In a well-functioning economy, increases in productivity may require a reduction in the number of factors utilized. Relative returns to the factors should then fall, not rise, to induce a movement elsewhere. And there is a further objection. In some activities productivity changes are slow or nonexistent. A rigid application of this doctrine would imply that people working in these areas should never have wage increases.

7. A final interpretation of the meaning of keeping wages in line with productivity is that wages should rise in general in line with gains in productivity in general. If output per man in the economy as a whole is growing at 4% a year, then everyone's wage should rise at the rate of 4% a year. In a well-functioning economy, however, relative wages should change to reflect changes in the relative scarcity of the factors of production, while this doctrine implies that relative wages should never change. Furthermore, some people undoubtedly feel that they are relatively underpaid, and we cannot expect them to agree to this rule. Others who have strong unions would be unwilling to accept less than average, or even average, increases in wages in order to permit the relative wages of the less well-paid to catch up.

7

International Trade and the Balance of Payments

The analysis, up to this point, has assumed away international trade. We do not live in a closed economy, however, and this makes a difference. The main purpose of this final chapter will be to show that difference. Three topics will be discussed. First, we shall introduce international trade (exports and imports) into national-income accounting. Then we shall examine the argument in favor of restricting imports to promote employment at home. Finally, we shall consider the meaning of a balance-of-payments problem and show why such a problem can interfere with the pursuit of full employment.

I. THE NNP STATEMENT WITH FOREIGN TRADE INCLUDED

Recall the statement of the net national product in the absence of international trade from Chapter 4. On the left side of that statement was recorded the disposition of the NNP. It was bought by households (C), by government (G), or, if by neither of these, it was absorbed by the business sector as additions to buildings, equipment, or inventories (NPDI). The existence of international trade introduces a further possibility; part of the NNP may have been exported. In the following statement of the NNP, exports (X) are, therefore, also recorded on the left.

The statement in Chapter 4 contained no imports. If C, G, and NPDI are to include all expenditures by households and government, as well as the net change in the capital stock, no matter where it came from, they must include imports. But imported goods and services are not part of our NNP; they are the result of productive activity in the rest of the world. In order not to exaggerate our production, it becomes necessary to subtract imports (M) from the sum of C, G, and NPDI. Imports (M), therefore, appear on the left side of the NNP Statement with a negative sign.

If, for example, expenditures by households (C) were $100 billion, $5 billion of which paid for imports; if government expenditures (G) were $10 billion, $2 billion of which covered imports; if buildings, equipment, and inventories increased $25 billion, $15 billion of which were imported; and if exports were $20 billions, the NNP would have been $133 billion, not $155 billion.

Table 7-1. Statement of the Net National Product

Consumption expenditures (C)	IBT
Government expenditures (G)	Wages and salaries
Net private domestic investment (NPDI)	Rent
	Interest
Exports (X)—imports (M)	Profits
NNP	NNP

The left side of the statement of the net national product can be written as an equation.

$$NNP = C + G + NPDI + X - M. \tag{7.1}$$

We also learned in Chapter 5 that

$$NNP = C + NPS + NT \tag{5.4}$$

Setting these two equations equal to each other, and eliminating C from both sides, we find that

$$G + NPDI + X - M = NPS + NT. \tag{7.2}$$

The difference between exports and imports, $X\text{-}M$, is defined to be net foreign investment (NFI). If NFI is added to $NPDI$

we obtain, dropping the *D* for domestic, net private investment (*NPI*). The statement of the net national product can, therefore, also be presented as shown in Table 7-2. And Eq. 7.2 becomes

$$G + NPI = NPS + NT. \qquad (7.3)$$

Table 7-2. Statement of the Net National Product

C	IBT
G	Wages and salaries
NPI	Rent
	Interest
	Profits
NNP	NNP

G minus *NT* can be defined as government investment (*GI*). If it is added to *NPI* we obtain, dropping the *P* for private, net investment (*NI*). Equation 7.3 then becomes

$$NI = NPS. \qquad (7.4)$$

QUESTIONS

1. Do C, G, and NPDI include only goods and services that were produced domestically?
2. If the NNP is $400 billion, C is $300 billion, G is $30 billion, NPDI is $40 billion, and M is $20 billion, what must X be?
3. If NPDI is $50 billion and NFI is minus $5 billion, what is NPI?
4. If NPI is $25 billion, G is $40 billion, and NT are $30 billion, what is NI?
5. Indicate, by referring to Eqs. 7.2, 7.3, and 7.4, the changes that would occur if the following transactions took place:
   (a) The government spends $200 million abroad.
   (b) Foreigners buy $2 billion worth of goods from us. Assume that the goods were in inventories and valued at $1.5 billion, and that the sellers must pay 50% of profits in income taxes.

II. EXPORTS, IMPORTS, AND AGGREGATE DEMAND

Aggregate demand for our output consists of the sum of consumption demand, investment demand, government demand, and exports demand (XD) minus import demand (MD). Import

Demand (MD) must be subtracted, because consumption, investment, and government demand include demand for goods and services produced abroad as well as domestically. Thus,

$$AD = CD + ID + GD + XD - MD. \qquad (7.5)$$

Since equilibrium requires that aggregate demand equal the *NNP*, it follows that in equilibrium

$$NNP = CD + ID + GD + XD - MD. \qquad (7.6)$$

If the other components of aggregate demand remain unchanged, Eq. 7.6 indicates that a reduction in *MD* raises equilibrium *NNP*. Here is a basis for the view, held by so many, that our nation would be better off if it followed the protectionist policy of restricting trade.

It is undoubtedly true that when the economy is suffering from a deficiency of aggregate demand and unemployment, an increase in aggregate demand would raise output and employment. If *MD* can be reduced so that domestic goods are demanded rather than foreign goods and if no other component of demand falls, then the economy would be better off. But one can accept this truth without becoming a protectionist. First, when the economy is operating at full employment, aggregate demand does not need stimulation. A protectionist policy will then be undesirable, since the economy will lose some of the benefits from an international division of labor. Second, exports and imports may also be interrelated, so that a reduction in imports induces a reduction in exports; attempts to stimulate exports or reduce imports may have no effect on aggregate demand. Furthermore, even if attempts to raise aggregate demand by reducing the demand for imports will be successful, it does not follow that this is a desirable policy. There may be far better ways to achieve this goal.

Consider the possibility that we and other nations are experiencing unemployment. Will a reduction in imports brought about by tariffs or import quotas increase aggregate demand and employment? If MD is reduced and no other component of aggregate demand falls, this will occur. But exports depend on imports. If we demand fewer goods from other countries, the aggregate demand for their output will decline; their NNP and employment will decrease. With less income, they well demand fewer goods and services, foreign as well as domestic. Their import demand will decrease; our export demand will fall. The original reduction in our demand for imports will, therefore, lead to a reduction in our export demand. It is possible that our exports will fall by less than the decline in our imports, so that the aggregate demand for our goods will rise somewhat. But if we achieve this result by switching demand away from foreign goods toward domestic goods, creating more employment at home, employment will fall in the rest of the world. The nations that are adversely affected by our protectionist policy are likely to retaliate or imitate our policy. When they do this, the employment gain following trade restrictions will be lost.

But even if retaliation or imitation did not occur, so that our aggregate demand could be increased by a program aimed at reducing imports, this would not be a desirable way to cure unemployment. If no other action to increase aggregate demand were possible, then a person with nationalistic feelings might favor a beggar-thy-neighbor policy. Our employment would grow at the expense of the rest of the world, but we are more important than they, he might feel. However, there are other means of increasing aggregate demand which do not require one to beggar his neighbor. The Federal Reserve authorities can reduce the cost and increase the availability of credit, or the Federal government can engage in deficit spending. By either road we can pursue the goal of full employment without creating an employment problem for others.

Not only should these latter methods of increasing aggregate demand for our goods be preferable because they do not create a problem for someone else, but they also help us further, since the benefits of world specialization would not be foregone in order to have full employment. International trade promotes specialization. With trade, each country tends to produce those goods in which it is *relatively* the most efficient or least inefficient. World production is increased. If we restrict trade to stimulate aggregate demand, even if it would achieve this objective, we forego, to some extent, the advantages of specialization and division of labor. Since there are other ways to maintain aggregate demand which do not have this undesirable side effect, trade reduction to increase aggregate demand should be rejected.

III. THE BALANCE-OF-PAYMENTS STATEMENT

A country's balance-of-payments statement records, for a certain period of time, all of its transactions with the rest of the world. International transactions consist of the purchase and sale of goods and services, payment and receipt of interest and dividends, borrowing and lending, and gifts.

Net unilateral remittances (net gifts to foreigners) is the difference between what was given to foreigners and what was received from them. If we gave the rest of the world more than we received from it, net unilateral remittances will be positive. If we receive more than given, it will be negative.

What do we give and what do we receive from the rest of the world? We give other nations exports of goods and services, the use of the capital that we have invested or lent abroad, as measured by the interest and dividends that we receive from foreigners, exports of financial assets (stocks, bonds, bank balances, and cash), and exports of gold. We receive from abroad imports of goods and services, the use of foreign capital that is invested in our country or lent to us, as measured by the interest and dividends we pay to foreigners, imports of financial assets (stocks, bonds, bank balances, and cash), and imports of gold. Thus, net unilateral remittances can be defined by the following equation:

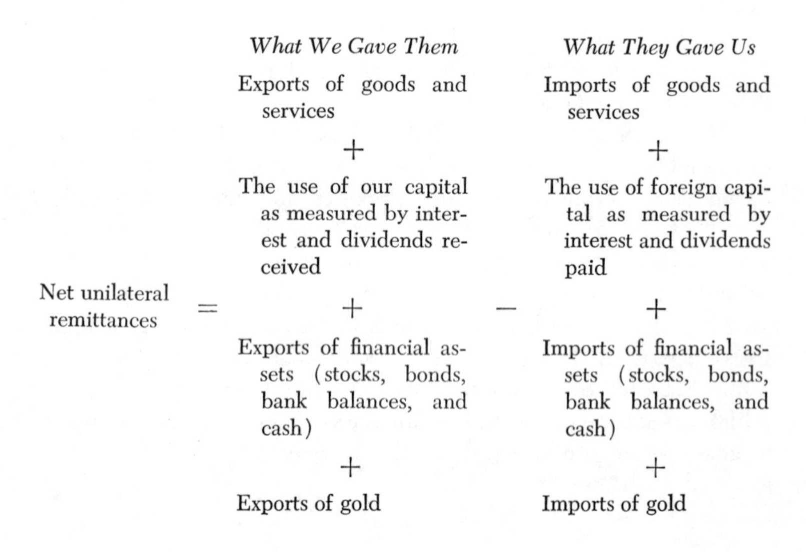

		What We Gave Them		*What They Gave Us*
		Exports of goods and services		Imports of goods and services
		+		+
		The use of our capital as measured by interest and dividends received		The use of foreign capital as measured by interest and dividends paid
Net unilateral remittances	=	+	−	+
		Exports of financial assets (stocks, bonds, bank balances, and cash)		Imports of financial assets (stocks, bonds, bank balances, and cash)
		+		+
		Exports of gold		Imports of gold

If, for example, we had the following information for a country for some period of time, we could compute the value of its net unilateral remittances.

Exports of goods and services	$40
Imports of goods and services	$38
Interest and dividends received	$ 6
Interest and dividends paid	$ 5
Exports of financial assets	$15
Imports of financial assets	$10
Exports of gold	$ 4
Imports of gold	$ 2

The country under consideration gave the rest of the world $40 in goods and services, the use of its capital for which $6 was paid, financial assets worth $15, and $4 worth of gold. This adds up to $65. It received goods and services worth $38, use of foreign capital for which it paid $5, financial assets worth $10, and $2 worth of gold. This adds up to $55. The value of all the things given the rest of the world was $65, while the value of all the things it received from the rest of the world was $55; net unilateral remittances were, therefore, $10.

Given the definition of net unilateral remittances, it is necessarily true that

Exports of goods and services		Imports of goods and services
+		+
Interest and dividends received		Interest and dividends paid
+	=	+
Exports of financial assets		Imports of financial assets
+		+
Exports of gold		Imports of gold
		+
		Net unilateral remittances

When this information is recorded in a statement with the items on the left side appearing on the left of that statement and the items on the right side on the right of the statement, a balance-of-payments statement is presented. Given the definition of net unilateral remittances, the two sides must sum to the same number. Using the information from the foregoing example, we attain the statement shown in Table 7-3.

Table 7-3. Balance-of-Payments Statement

Exports of goods and services	$40	Imports of goods and services	$38
Interest and dividends received	6	Interest and dividends paid	5
Exports of financial assets	15	Imports of financial assets	10
Exports of gold	4	Imports of gold	2
		Net unilateral remittances	10
	$65		$65

There are many ways in which the information contained in a balance-of-payments statement can be arranged. Instead of showing interest and dividends received and interest and dividends paid separately, one can be subtracted from the other and we can record only the net amount. If interest and dividends paid are subtracted from interest and dividends received, we have net interest and dividends received. Imports of financial assets can be subtracted from exports of financial assets and net capital movements can be recorded in their place. Similarly, gold imports can be subtracted from gold exports and net gold movements recorded. The balance-of-payments statement could then be presented as shown in Table 7-4.

Table 7-4. Balance-of-Payments Statement

Exports of goods and services	$40	Imports of goods and services	$38
Net interest and dividends received	1	Net unilateral remittances	10
Net capital movements	5		
Net gold movements	2		
	$48		$48

QUESTIONS

1. Why are dividends and interest received listed as something given to the rest of the world, rather than received from them?
2. Assume that the following information represents the international transactions of a country for a period of time:

Exports of goods and services	$38
Imports of goods and services	40
Interest and dividends received	6
Interest and dividends paid	6
Exports of financial assets	10

Imports of financial assets	15
Exports of gold	2
Imports of gold	4

(a) What did this nation give to the rest of the world and what did it receive from the rest of the world?

(b) What were net unilateral remittances? Explain what it means when net unilateral remittances is a negative number.

(c) Prepare a balance-of-payments statement similar to the one shown in Table 7-3.

(d) Prepare a balance-of-payments statement similar to the one shown in Table 7-4.

3. Explain why a balance-of-payments statement must always balance.

IV. BALANCE-OF-PAYMENTS PROBLEMS

Economists and others often speak of balance-of-payments problems. What can be meant by this? Clearly it does not mean that one side of a balance-of-payments statement does not equal the other, for they are necessarily equal. What then does it mean?

To understand the nature of a balance-of-payments problem, one must understand the international monetary system. The United States is on a restricted gold standard. Although gold is not used domestically as a medium of exchange, it does serve as money internationally. Our government will buy all gold offered to it at $35 an ounce, and it will sell gold at that price, except to U.S. citizens for hoarding purposes. Other countries have also tied their money to gold; they will buy and sell it for fixed amounts of their money. When two countries are prepared to buy and sell gold at definite prices, the value of the money of any one of the countries is fixed in terms of the other.

If the United States will buy and sell gold at $35 an ounce while some other country will buy and sell gold at 70 pesos an ounce, then in equilibrium $1 will buy 2 pesos. If the price of a peso tends to rise above 50¢, ignoring transportation costs, banks and other foreign exchange dealers will buy gold with dollars, transport the gold to Pesoland, and then sell it for pesos. The pesos will, in turn, be sold for dollars, reducing the value of a peso until it costs no more than 50¢. To take an example, assume that the price of a peso is 60¢. A person with $350,000 can obtain

10,000 ounces of gold. If the gold is sent to Pesoland, it can be sold to the government there for 700,000 pesos. The pesos could then be sold for dollars. If one peso is selling for 60¢, then 700,000 pesos will bring $420,000. By buying gold in the United States for dollars, transporting the gold to Pesoland, selling it here for pesos, and then selling the pesos for dollars, $350,000 can be turned into $420,000. The profitability of this transaction will not be overlooked by foreign exchange dealers and the supply of pesos for dollars will rise. As the pesos are offered for sale, the value of a peso will fall and will continue to fall until a peso sells for 50¢.

If, on the other hand, a peso can be bought for less than 50¢, for instance, 40¢, a reverse flow of gold will occur. Then 700,000 pesos can be turned into 10,000 ounces of gold. The gold can then be brought to the United States and converted into $350,000. With the peso selling for 40¢, the original 700,000 pesos can be turned into 875,000. Again the profitability of this transaction will be noticed by foreign exchange dealers. As gold enters the United States and the dollars received for it are sold for pesos, the value of the dollar in terms of the peso will fall; the value of the peso will rise. The rise in the value of the peso will continue until it is selling for 50¢.

With each currency selling for the correct price, given the amount of gold into which it is convertible, a flow of gold is still possible. If the demand for pesos at 50¢ each is greater than the supply, gold will leave the United States in order to obtain the pesos needed to meet the demand. We demand foreign exchange in order to import goods and services, pay interest and dividends, import financial assets, and make gifts to foreigners. They supply us with foreign exchange in order to buy our exports, pay us interest and dividends, buy financial assets from us, and make us gifts. When the demand for foreign exchange exceeds the supply, we have a *balance-of-payments deficit*. If the monetary authorities took no action whatsoever, we would lose gold. We need not lose gold immediately if they borrow from other countries to prevent gold losses; we can, therefore, have a balance-of-payments deficit without actually losing gold.

A balance-of-payments deficit need not be a concern if we believe, in spite of gold losses, that we have sufficient gold. A *balance-of-payments problem* exists when there is fear that balance-of-payments deficits will be so great that we will run out of gold.

A nation can have what you and I may believe is a relatively large stock of gold and yet have a balance-of-payments problem. Everyone may not agree with us. If many people believe that our gold stock is not sufficient for us to continue to maintain convertibility of dollars into gold at $35 an ounce, we may have to change the price. If the price goes to $70 and the gold value of the peso remains unchanged, then instead of $1 equaling 2 pesos, $1 will equal 1 peso. The dollar is devalued; it is only worth one half as much in terms of pesos. People who expected this to happen shortly would have a great incentive to buy pesos now for dollars, hold the pesos, and then convert them back into dollars after the devaluation. Now $1000 will buy 2000 pesos. Later on, the 2000 pesos will be convertible back into $2000.

The possible drain on our gold stock could be enormous if devaluation was widely expected. A person could use all of his cash and bank balances, could sell all of his stocks and bonds, could sell his house, and could borrow from others in order to buy pesos for dollars. A foreigner who believed that the dollar was going to be devalued would get rid of any bank balances he had in the United States, sell any securities he owned that were saleable in the United States, and borrow whatever he could in the United States, converting all of the receipts into pesos. If there are only a few persons who believe that we will devalue, there would be no particular problem. But if the view becomes general, so much gold will leave the United States that we could be forced to abandon our commitment to give an ounce of gold for $35. We could be forced into the position that was anticipated by the speculators.

Although a deficit in the balance of payments need not be troublesome, those responsible for managing the international monetary mechanism are almost inevitably going to worry if we are, in fact, losing gold or tending to lose it. You never know when there will be a run on the dollar, and a balance-of-payments deficit could trigger one.

The existence of a gold stock that is much smaller than the possible claims against it is similar in some respects to our fractional-reserve banking system in which there are far more deposits payable on demand than there is currency to pay them.

Neither of these situations need present a problem. People can have claims against gold without exercising them, as they can have demand deposits payable in currency without asking for the currency. But the potential for real trouble is always present. If depositors believe that the bank cannot pay in currency, they would immediately demand it. Similarly, if it becomes widely believed that the United States can no longer maintain its committment to pay gold, more gold will be demanded than we have.

The analogy between the international monetary system and our commercial banking system can be carried no further. Today, if depositors begin draining currency from our banking system, no crisis need occur. The Federal Reserve Banks now have the power to create all the new currency needed to lend to the banks. But a run on gold is not so easily handled, since there is no institution in the world that can create it. If the demands for gold exceed our gold stock, we can turn to the International Monetary Fund, where we have a limited drawing right, and we can borrow to some unpredictable degree from foreign central banks and governments, but there is no guarantee that we can maintain our commitment to pay gold. The International Monetary Fund does not have as much power to prevent an international monetary crisis as the Federal Reserve System has to prevent a domestic one.

At the end of the Second World War the gold stock of the United States seemed large and it tended to grow. There was much talk of a world dollar shortage, which meant that other nations were unable to obtain all the dollars they wanted. Sometime in the 1950s, however, this situation reversed itself; the United States began to accumulate increasing claims against its gold stock and the stock actually began to diminish. Fears became increasingly great that unless some government actions were taken we might experience a run on our gold stock. In 1966, although some measures have been taken, the problem was still with us.

QUESTIONS

1. If today the United States holds 500,000,000 ounces of gold, what is the value of our gold stock?

2. Assume that the United States will freely buy and sell gold at $35 an ounce and that some other country will freely buy and sell it at 105 drachmas an ounce. Ignore transportation costs.
   (a) What would drachmas cost in dollars in equilibrium? Explain carefully, indicating what would happen if drachmas were more or less expensive.
   (b) Assuming that the demand for drachmas equals the supply initially, list the possible changes which could occur that would lead to a greater demand than supply of drachmas?
   (c) What will happen if the demand for drachmas exceeds the supply?
3. What is meant by a balance-of-payments deficit?
4. Distinguish between a balance-of-payments problem and a balance-of-payments deficit.
5. If many people believe that the United States is about to run out of gold and will, therefore, shortly raise its price, what will they do and what will be the consequences of their actions?
6. "The International Monetary Fund has as much power to prevent a run on gold as the Federal Reserve Banks have to prevent a run on our banks." Comment.

V. FLEXIBLE EXCHANGE RATES AS A SOLUTION TO BALANCE-OF-PAYMENTS PROBLEMS

Balance-of-payments problems will no longer trouble us if we will only make a complete break with the international gold standard. The dollar does not have to be convertible into gold. If the United States abandons its commitment to buy and sell gold at a fixed price, foreign exchange rates will be determined by supply and demand. If the demand for pesos exceeds the supply of pesos when pesos cost 50¢ each, the price of pesos will rise until the demand does equal the supply. Similarly, if the supply of pesos exceeds the demand, the price of pesos will fall until supply and demand are equal. An excess demand for foreign exchange will not reduce our monetary gold stock, since we will not pay out gold. An excess supply of foreign exchange does not increase our gold stock, since we will not buy it. Balance-of-payments problems will be a thing of the past.

Although it must be admitted that the introduction of flexible exchange rates and complete abandonment of the gold standard will eliminate the possibility of balance of payments, many critics of flexible exchange rates believe that this preventive cure is worse than the disease. They argue that, under a system of flexible rates, the variations in the exchange rates will be unduly great and these fluctuations will reduce the amount of trade. We shall no longer have balance-of-payments problems, but we shall have something worse, unstable exchange rates and less international trade.

It is difficult to predict the degree to which exchange rates will fluctuate if they are free to be determined by supply and demand. Speculation in exchange rates is possible and can be destabilizing, although it need not be. It is also impossible to known how much international trade will be reduced by fluctuating exchange rates. Businessmen might be less certain of the prices they will get for their sales abroad and avoid, to some extent, dealing in international markets. But the extent to which this would reduce international specialization and exchange below some optimum is unpredictable.

Whether the objection to flexible exchange rates is legitimate or not, the United States is committed to maintaining international convertibility into gold. At the moment, the suggestion that we leave the gold standard and have flexible exchange rates is not considered seriously by those in authority.

QUESTIONS

1. Under a system of freely flexible exchange rates in which the United States Government will neither buy nor sell gold, what will happen if the demand for drachmas exceeds their supply?
2. Why do some people believe that international trade will be significantly reduced if we abandon the gold standard and permit exchange rates to fluctuate?

VI. OTHER SOLUTIONS TO BALANCE-OF-PAYMENTS PROBLEMS

Aside from introducing a system of flexible exchange rates by abandoning the commitment to convert dollars into gold, there are other things that can be tried to correct a balance-of-payments problem. If we currently are losing gold or having to borrow to prevent gold losses, a lack of confidence in the dollar may occur which can be corrected only by eliminating the current deficit in the balance of payments. The question that will concern us, therefore, is what can be done to stop gold losses.

Consider the balance-of-payments statement in Table 7-4. Net gold movements appear on the left side, having been defined as gold exports minus gold imports. It is this number that we desire to reduce; gold exports must fall or gold imports rise. How can this be done? Since the two sides of a balance-of-payments statement add up to the same number, if net gold movements are to decline then some other item on the statement must also change, either up or down depending on which side it appears. An increase in export of goods and services, a decrease in imports of goods and services, an increase in net interest and dividends received, a decrease in net unilateral transfers, or an increase in net capital movements will achieve this objective. It seems natural, therefore, to conclude that a balance-of-payments problem can be cured by adopting policies that will affect imports, exports, unilateral transfers, or capital movements. If imports can be reduced, then gold flows can be reduced. But this does not necessarily follow. A policy aimed at reducing imports might reduce exports and leave gold movements unchanged. Let us explore this possibility in more detail.

It is possible by granting subsidies to exporters or by introducing higher tariffs or more limiting quotas on imports to increase exports and reduce imports, at least initially. Such a policy will reduce gold flows, however, only if foreign nations fail to retaliate or imitate our policy. If they do what we do, there will be no permanent change in gold movements. We end up with the same balance-of-payments problem and an additional undesirable condition, an interference with the free flow of goods and services internationally.

It is possible to stimulate exports and reduce imports without resorting to subsidies, tariffs, or quotas. An alternative is to reduce aggregate demand in the United States. If the government raises taxes or reduces its demand for goods and services, aggregate demand will fall by some multiple of this and imports will be affected. Fewer goods and services will be bought, including imported ones. The reduction in demand might also have some effect on our prices, pushing them downward. Lower prices in the United States relative to those abroad will encourage foreigners to buy more of our goods and domestic exporters to push their sales abroad.

Similarly, imports and exports can be altered by actions of the Federal Reserve authorities to increase the cost and reduce the availability of credit. Investment demand and, therefore, aggregate demand will be reduced. Imports will fall off and exports will rise, for the reasons given in the previous paragraph.

But we must not conclude that a balance-of-payments deficit will be corrected by reducing our aggregate demand until we have considered foreign repercussions. If we buy fewer goods from foreign countries and if we compete harder with them, taking away markets from their firms, aggregate demand will fall in the rest of the world. But when they demand fewer goods, our exports decline. Furthermore, if foreign suppliers become more competitive through lower prices, resulting from the reduction in their aggregate demand, our imports will rise. The initial reduction in our imports and increase in our exports will have repercussions abroad which will reverse, to some degree, the original changes. It is not obvious, therefore, that the attempt to solve a balance-of-payments problem by reducing demand will actually achieve that result. And, if it does tend to eliminate the problem, there is no guarantee that the reduction in trade will not have to be large to reduce a small deficit.

Increasing the cost and reducing the availability of credit will have effects other than those on imports and exports of goods and services. They will also affect net capital movements. Restrictive monetary policy will raise interest rates. With interest rates in the United States higher than before, we will buy fewer foreign securities and they will buy more of ours. Net capital movements on the left side of our balance-of-payments statement will rise. Given the other items unchanged, gold exports will fall. But again one must be careful to avoid assuming that a potential gold loss of $1 billion can be eliminated simply by some action to cause an initial change of $1 billion in some item on the balance-of-payments statement. All of the items on a balance-of-payments statement are interrelated. If we invest less abroad, foreigners will demand fewer goods and services. They will buy fewer imports, and our exports will fall. In addition, as their firms experience a reduction in demand, foreigners will, to some extent, become more competitive by reducing prices; our imports will rise.

But granting that restrictive fiscal or monetary policy will have the net effect of reducing a balance-of-payments problem, it by no means follows that either action should be taken. If the economy is not suffering from excessive demand, then a reduction in aggregate demand will reduce NNP and create unemployment. We are faced with a dilemma. Maintenance of full employment suggests that government demand, taxes, and credit conditions remain unchanged. Yet a desire to solve the balance-of-payments problem suggests that restrictive fiscal or monetary policy be established.

Let us consider one final possible solution: reduce net unilateral remittances. Some students of international monetary problems have suggested that we reduce foreign aid in the belief that a reduction in this item on the right side of the balance-of-payments statement will reduce net gold movements on the left. But it is the belief of our government that this aid is important, if not vital, to our interests. Assuming that a reduction in foreign aid will correct the situation, it does not follow that this is the solution to be taken. Again it is not clear just how much of a reduction in net gold flows will follow from a reduction in aid. If foreign countries receive less aid from the United States they will spend less on imports. A reduction in net unilateral remittances will to some extent, if not to the same extent, reduce our exports.

The United States government has taken a number of steps to reduce our balance-of-payments deficit in order to prevent a run on the dollar. Dependents of servicemen have been discouraged from living abroad. PXs have been required to minimize their purchases of foreign goods. Fullbright Fellows are required to travel on American-owned ships. A tax has been placed on new purchases of foreign securities and voluntary limits placed on the amount of foreign lending. The duty-free allowance permitted Americans returning from abroad has been reduced. If the situation become more serious, further restrictions on the right to travel, to import, and to invest abroad will undoubtedly be introduced.

If balance-of-payments problems can be prevented only by

restricting travel, foreign investment, and trade, there is less justification for continuing our commitment to the limited gold standard. The major justification for keeping dollars convertible into gold is the belief that international trade will be reduced below some optimum if exchange rates are left to find their own level by supply and demand. But if trade must be restricted, it is less clear that the present system is the best one.

QUESTIONS

1. As a mere matter of accounting, what does a reduction in net gold movements on the left side of the balance-of-payments statement as it appears in Table 7-4 require in terms of the other items on that statement?
2. Ignoring foreign repercussions, why will export subsidies, tariffs, and import quotas tend to reduce a balance-of-payments deficit?
3. Why is the extent not clear to which subsidies, tariffs, or import quotas will reduce net gold exports, when foreign repercussions are considered?
4. Ignoring foreign repercussions, why will restrictive monetary and fiscal policy tend to reduce a balance-of-payments deficit?
5. When foreign repercussions are considered, why is the extent unclear to which restrictive monetary and fiscal policy will reduce a balance-of-payments deficit?
6. Why might restrictive monetary policy not be undertaken to cure a balance-of-payments deficit, even if it is believed that it will work?
7. What is the objection to eliminating a balance-of-payments deficit by reducing foreign aid?

VII. CONCLUSION

In this and the preceding chapter we have shown that there may be a conflict in the objectives of public policy. Most Americans appear to believe that it is desirable to have full employment, price stability, a fixed price of gold, freedom to travel, to trade, and to lend internationally, a small national debt, and an equitable distribution of income. And there are undoubtedly others that many could agree to. We have discussed the means that we have to achieve some of them, but have suggested that we may be unable to achieve all of them simultaneously. If they cannot all be achieved simultaneously, then painful choices are necessary.

The main attention in this book has been on the problem of maintaining full employment. We have shown how unemployment can occur and how it can be remedied. But we have not shown that it can always be prevented without the sacrifice of other goals.

VIII. SUMMARY

1. This chapter had three purposes: (1) to introduce international trade into national income accounting, (2) to examine the argument for restricting imports in order to promote employment at home, and (3) to consider the nature of a balance-of-payments problem and show why it may be difficult to correct without creating unemployment.

2. The NNP consists of the sum of C, G, NPDI, and X minus M. M must be subtracted since C, G, and NPDI contain imported goods and services, which are not part of our production.

3. NFI is the difference between X and M. NFI plus NPDI is equal to NPI. G minus NT can be defined as GI. GI plus NPI can be defined as NI.

4. It follows from the definitions and the components of the NNP that NI is necessarily equal to NPS.

5. AD for output consists of CD, ID, GD, XD minus MD. MD must be subtracted because CD, ID and GD include the demand for goods produced in the rest of the world.

6. A reduction in MD by higher tariffs or lower import quotas will increase initially the AD for our goods and services. But exports and imports are interrelated. If we reduce our imports, AD will fall abroad, and foreign countries will buy less from us; our exports will decline. Foreign nations will also retaliate or imitate our beggar-thy-neighbor policy. It is not clear, therefore, that unemployment can be reduced by raising tariffs or reducing import quotas. And, even if reducing imports will create jobs domestically, there are better ways to achieve full employment.

7. Net unilateral remittances (net gifts to foreigners) is the difference between what we give to the rest of the world and what they give us. A balance-of-payments statement follows from this definition. One side consists of what we give the rest of the world, while the other side consists of what we receive

from the rest of the world plus net unilateral remittances. This statement can be rearranged many ways by introducing new definitions.

8. A balance-of-payments problem cannot mean that one side of a balance-of-payments statement does not equal the other; they are necessarily equal. A balance-of-payments problem exists when there is fear that we may run out of gold. Actual losses of gold or the need to borrow to prevent losses of gold may lead to a balance-of-payments problem. If many people expect that the United States will have to increase the amount that it will pay for gold, there will be a flight from the dollar, and that which is expected will come about.

9. Balance-of-payments problems could not occur if we abandoned our remaining attachment to gold. Exchange rates could be determined by supply and demand rather than by the amount of gold into which various currencies are convertible. Some argue that this is a poor alternative, however. Exchange rates will constantly fluctuate under a free system and businessmen will avoid dealing in foreign markets. International trade will decline.

10. Numerous things can be tried to eliminate a loss or tendency for a loss of gold in order to prevent a balance-of-payments problem from leading to a crisis. Exports can be increased and imports reduced by subsidies, tariffs, and quotas. It is not certain, however, that this will reduce net gold exports, once foreign repercussions are considered. Even if it would work, it is undesirable because it interferes with the freedom to trade.

11. Exports can be stimulated and imports reduced by any policy that reduces aggregate demand. But, again, when foreign repercussions are considered, it is not clear how effective this policy will be.

12. International capital flows can be altered by raising interest rates in our country relative to those abroad; the initial effect of this is to reduce gold exports. But the amount that we lend abroad determines, to some degree, the amount that foreign countries buy from us. If we lend less, we shall export less.

13. A policy of reducing aggregate demand and raising interest rates will lead to unemployment unless there is excessive demand to begin with.

14. Net unilateral remittances can be reduced by giving a small amount of foreign aid. But, again, the effects of this action are obscure. Those who receive the foreign aid will have to buy less from us because they have less to spend. Net unilateral remittances decline, but so do exports of goods and services. It must also be remembered that foreign aid is given because we believe it is necessary and desirable. It will be unfortunate if we have to abandon foreign aid simply because of a balance-of-payments problem.

15. This and the previous chapter have shown that it may be difficult, if not impossible, to achieve all desirable economic objectives. This book's main concern has been with the problem of unemployment. We may be able to come close to having full employment continually, but it is not certain that the pursuit of this objective will be costless. Economic policy has other objectives, and if we are to aim for full employment one or more of them may have to be sacrificed.

Index